THE COLD WAR

History SparkNotes

SPARKNOTES is a registered trademark of SparkNotes LLC

Spark Educational Publishing
A Division of Barnes & Noble Publishing
120 Fifth Avenue
New York, NY 10011
www.sparknotes.com

ISBN 1-4114-0422-X

Please submit all comments and questions or report errors to *www.sparknotes.com/errors*.

Printed and bound in the United States

CONTENTS

OVERVIEW

R ivalry between the United States and the Soviet Union for control over the postwar world emerged before World War II had even ended. U.S. presidents Franklin D. Roosevelt and Harry S Truman and Soviet premier Joseph Stalin never really trusted one another, even while working together to defeat the Nazis. This mutual mistrust actually began as far back as 1917, when the United States refused to recognize the new Bolshevik government after the Russian Revolution. Stalin also resented the fact that the United States and Great Britain had not shared nuclear weapons research with the Soviet Union during the war and was unhappy with the countries' initial unwillingness to engage the Germans on a second front in order to take pressure off of the Soviets. Additionally, Stalin was irked by the fact that Truman had offered postwar relief loans to Great Britain but not to the USSR.

Important ideological differences separated the two countries as well, especially during the postwar years, when American foreign policy officials took it upon themselves to spread democracy across the globe. This goal conflicted drastically with the Russian revolutionaries' original desire to overthrow capitalism. Having been invaded by Germany twice in the last fifty years, Soviet leaders also wanted to restructure Europe so that a buffer existed between the Germans and the Soviet border. Both the United States and the USSR believed that their respective survival was at stake, and each was therefore prepared to take any steps to win. As a result, both countries found themselves succumbing to the classic prisoners' dilemma: working together would produce the best result, but with everything to lose, neither side could risk trusting the other.

At the same time, however, both the United States and the USSR did much to prevent the Cold War from escalating, as both countries knew how devastating a nuclear war would be. Truman, for example, kept the Korean War limited by refusing to use nuclear weapons against North Korea and China, aware that doing so would force the USSR to retaliate. President Dwight D. Eisenhower kept his distance from the Hungarian Revolution in 1956, knowing full well that the USSR would not tolerate interference in Eastern Europe. Likewise, the Soviet Union made sacrifices to keep the war "cold" by backing down from the Cuban missile crisis. Many Cold War historians believe that both countries worked hard to keep conflicts limited and used tacit signaling techniques to communicate goals, fears, concerns, intensions, and counteractions.

The Cold War had an enormous impact on the United States politically, socially, and economically. In addition to spawning fear-induced Red hunts and McCarthyism in the late 1940s and early 1950s, the Cold War also shaped U.S. presidents' political agendas. Eisenhower, for example, sought to reduce government spending at home in order to halt what he called "creeping socialism" and to save money for more urgent needs such as defense. Kennedy's New Frontier inspired patriotic fervor and visions of new hope in American youth. Even Eisenhower's farewell warning of a growing military-industrial complex within the United States, which would come to dominate American political thinking, proved to be eerily accurate during the Vietnam War era the following decade. At the same time, federal dollars feeding this complex helped produce one of the greatest economic booms in world history.

The question as to whether the United States or the USSR was more to blame for starting the Cold War has produced heated debate among twentieth-century historians. For years, most historians placed blame squarely on Soviet shoulders and helped perpetuate the notion that Americans wanted merely to expand freedom and democracy. More recent historians, however, have accused President Truman of inciting the Cold War with his acerbic language and public characterization of the Soviet Union as the greatest threat to the free world. Although conflict between the two powers was arguably inevitable, the escalation into a full "hot" war and the attendant threat of nuclear annihilation might have been avoidable.

SUMMARY OF EVENTS

POSTWAR TENSION

In many ways, the Cold War began even before the guns fell silent in Germany and in the Pacific in 1945. Suspicion and mistrust had defined U.S.-Soviet relations for decades and resurfaced as soon as the alliance against Adolf Hitler was no longer necessary. Competing ideologies and visions of the postwar world prevented U.S. president **Harry S Truman** and Soviet premier **Joseph Stalin** from working together.

Stalin intended to destroy Germany's industrial capabilities in order to prevent the country from remilitarizing and wanted Germany to pay outrageous sums in war reparations. Moreover, he wanted to erect pro-Soviet governments throughout Eastern Europe to protect the USSR from any future invasions. Truman, however, wanted exactly the opposite. He believed that only industrialization and democracy in Germany and throughout the continent would ensure postwar stability. Unable to compromise or find common ground, the world's two remaining superpowers inevitably clashed.

TRUMAN'S POSTWAR VISION

Truman worked tirelessly to clean up the postwar mess and establish a new international order. He helped create the **World Bank** and the **International Monetary Fund (IMF)** and funded the rebuilding of Japan under General **Douglas MacArthur**. After prosecuting Nazi war criminals at the **Nuremberg trials**, Truman in 1947 also outlined the **Marshall Plan**, which set aside more than $10 billion for the rebuilding and reindustrialization of Germany. The Marshall Plan was so successful that factories in Western Europe were exceeding their prewar production levels within just a few years.

STALIN'S POSTWAR VISION

Although Stalin joined with the United States in founding the **United Nations**, he fought Truman on nearly every other issue. He protested the Marshall Plan as well as the formation of the World Bank and IMF. In defiance, he followed through on his plan to create a buffer between the Soviet Union and Germany by setting up pro-Communist governments in Poland and other Eastern European countries. As a result, the so-called **iron curtain** soon divided East from West in Europe. Stalin also tried unsuccessfully to drive French, British, and

3

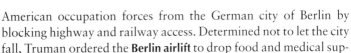

American occupation forces from the German city of Berlin by blocking highway and railway access. Determined not to let the city fall, Truman ordered the **Berlin airlift** to drop food and medical supplies for starving Berliners.

CONTAINMENT

The Berlin crisis, as well as the formation of the **Eastern bloc** of Soviet-dominated countries in Eastern Europe, caused foreign policy officials in Washington to believe that the United States needed to check Soviet influence abroad in order to prevent the further spread of Communism. In 1947, Truman incorporated this desire for **containment** into his **Truman Doctrine**, which vowed to support free nations fighting Communism. He and Congress then pledged $400 million to fighting Communist revolutionaries in Greece and Turkey. In 1949, Truman also convinced the Western European powers to join the **North Atlantic Treaty Organization (NATO)**, so that they might mutually defend themselves against the danger of Soviet invasion. Threatened, the USSR sponsored a similar treaty of its own in Eastern Europe, called the **Warsaw Pact**, in 1955.

TRUMAN AT HOME

In the domestic policy arena, Truman signed the **National Security Act** in 1947 to restructure America's defenses for the new Communist threat. The act reorganized the military under the new office of the **secretary of defense** and the new **Joint Chiefs of Staff**. It also created the **National Security Council** to advise the president on global affairs and the **Central Intelligence Agency** to conduct espionage. Truman's leadership in confronting the Soviet Union and rebuilding Europe convinced Democrats to nominate him again for the 1948 election. His **Fair Deal** domestic policies and support for civil rights, however, divided the Republican Party and nearly cost Truman the election.

RED HUNTS

Developments in Eastern Europe, the fall of **China** to Communist revolutionaries in 1949, and the Soviet Union's development of nuclear weapons terrified Americans, who feared that Communists would try to infiltrate or attack the United States from within. Congressman **Richard M. Nixon** and the **House Un-American Activities Committee** led the earliest **Red hunts** for Communists in the government, which culminated with the prosecution of federal employee **Alger Hiss** and the executions of suspected spies **Julius and Ethel**

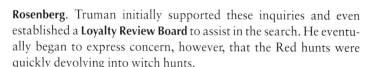

Rosenberg. Truman initially supported these inquiries and even established a **Loyalty Review Board** to assist in the search. He eventually began to express concern, however, that the Red hunts were quickly devolving into witch hunts.

THE KOREAN WAR

Cold War tensions between the United States and the USSR eventually exploded in **Korea** when Soviet-backed North Korea invaded South Korea in 1950. Determined not to let Communism spread in East Asia, Truman quadrupled military spending and ordered General MacArthur to retake the southern half of the peninsula. MacArthur succeeded and then pushed the North Koreans almost up to the Chinese border. Threatened, over a million soldiers from Communist China poured into Korea, forcing MacArthur to retreat back to the **38th parallel**, which had originally divided North Korea from South Korea.

When MacArthur began to criticize Truman publicly for his unwillingness to use nuclear weapons in Korea, Truman was forced to fire his top general for insubordination. United States forces remained entrenched at the 38th parallel for two more years, at the cost of more than 50,000 American lives. Both sides declared a cease-fire only after the new U.S. president, **Dwight D. Eisenhower**, threatened to use nuclear weapons in 1953.

POSTWAR PROSPERITY

Eisenhower's election in 1952 ushered in an unprecedented era of economic growth and prosperity in the United States. The average national income doubled during the 1950s and then doubled again the following decade, primarily due to continued defense spending and to the 1944 **Montgomery G.I. Bill**, which helped returning veterans buy homes and go back to school. The postwar *"baby boom"* contributed to population growth, while the **Great Migration** of African-Americans to northern cities, **"white flight"** from the cities to the suburbs, and the rush to the **Sun Belt** altered population demographics. By 1960, most American families had a car, a television, and a refrigerator and owned their own home. Popular television **sitcoms** like *Leave It to Beaver* and *Ozzie and Harriet* glamorized suburbia and consumerism.

CREEPING SOCIALISM

"Ike" Eisenhower had entered the White House determined to block the creation of new social welfare programs, which he called "creeping socialism." He did not, however, cut federal funding from existing New Deal programs. In fact, he expanded **Social Security** and the **Federal Housing Administration** and even set aside tens of millions of dollars for the creation of the first **interstates** under the **Federal Highway Act**. Still a conservative, though, Eisenhower refused to endorse the blossoming **civil rights movement** and signed the **Landrum-Griffin Act**, also known as the Labor-Management Reporting and Disclosure Act, in the wake of numerous **AFL-CIO** labor union scandals in the mid-1950s.

McCarthyism

First-term Wisconsin Republican senator **Joseph McCarthy**, meanwhile, exploded onto the national political scene in 1950, when he accused more than 200 federal employees of being Communists. Even though McCarthy had no proof to support these claims, Americans supported his endeavors to find more "Soviet agents" hiding in Washington. Thousands of former New Dealers and Red-hunt critics from all walks of life were wrongfully persecuted. McCarthy's influence eventually waned after he humiliated himself during the nationally televised **Army-McCarthy hearings** in 1954.

Ike's New Look

In addition to halting "creeping socialism" at home, Eisenhower also wanted to **"roll back"** Communist advances abroad. Along with Vice President **Richard M. Nixon** and Secretary of State **John Foster Dulles**, Eisenhower devised a **New Look** at foreign policy that emphasized the use of nuclear weapons, rather than conventional weapons and troops, to contain Communism. Eisenhower threatened the USSR with **"massive retaliation,"** or nuclear war, against Soviet aggression or the spread of Communism.

Eisenhower also made full use of the newly created **CIA** to help overthrow unfriendly governments in developing countries. He resolved the **Suez crisis** peacefully before it led to war and committed American funds to fighting **Ho Chi Minh**'s pro-Communist forces in **Vietnam** after the French defeat at Dien Bien Phu in 1954. The Soviet launch of the Sputnik satellites in 1957 started the **space race**, prompting Eisenhower to create the **National Aeronautics and Space Administration (NASA)**, and sign the **National Defense Education Act**. In his farewell address in 1961, he warned Americans of the growing **military-industrial complex** that threatened to restrict civil liberties and dominate American foreign policy making.

KENNEDY AND THE NEW FRONTIER

Facing term limits, Eisenhower endorsed Vice President **Richard Nixon** for the Republican presidential nomination in 1960. Democrats countered with World War II hero and Massachusetts senator **John F. Kennedy**. After a close race, Kennedy defeated Nixon, thanks in large part to the African-American vote and Kennedy's polished performance in the first-ever **televised presidential debates**.

As president, Kennedy pushed for a package of new social welfare spending programs that he called the **New Frontier**. Hoping to inspire a new generation of young Americans, he told them to "ask not what your country can do for you; ask what you can do for your country." Republicans and conservative southern Democrats, however, blocked most New Frontier legislation in Congress.

FLEXIBLE RESPONSE

Because Eisenhower's threat of "massive retaliation" had proved too stringent and binding, Kennedy and his foreign policy team devised a new doctrine of **"flexible response"** designed to give the president more options to fight Communism.

In addition, Kennedy committed thousands of American troops to South Vietnam to support **Ngo Dinh Diem**'s corrupt regime but claimed the troops were merely "military advisors." In Latin America, Kennedy took a different approach, funneling millions of dollars into the **Alliance for Progress** to thwart Communists by ending poverty. Despite the new doctrine, Kennedy was unable to prevent Soviet premier **Nikita Khrushchev** from constructing the **Berlin Wall** in 1961.

THE CUBAN CRISES

Kennedy's greatest Cold War challenge came in **Cuba**. Hoping to topple Cuba's new pro-Communist revolutionary leader, **Fidel Castro**, Kennedy authorized the CIA to train and arm a force of more than 1,000 Cuban exiles and sent them to invade Cuba in the spring of 1961. When this **Bay of Pigs invasion** failed embarrassingly, Kennedy authorized several unsuccessful assassination attempts against Castro. Outraged, Castro turned to the USSR for economic aid and protection.

Khrushchev capitalized on the opportunity and placed several nuclear missiles in Cuba. Kennedy consequently blockaded the island nation, pushing the United States and the USSR to the brink of nuclear war. Khrushchev ended the terrifying **Cuban missile crisis** when he agreed to remove the missiles in exchange for an end to the blockade. Kennedy also removed American missiles from Turkey and agreed to work on reducing Cold War tensions. Tragically, Kennedy was assassinated in late 1963, just as tensions were rising in Vietnam—which would prove to be the next, and most costly, theater of the Cold War.

KEY PEOPLE & TERMS

PEOPLE

ALLEN DULLES
The director of the **CIA** under Eisenhower, who advocated extensive use of **covert operations**. Most notable among Dulles's initiatives were U.S.-sponsored coups in **Iran** in 1953 and **Guatemala** in 1954, which installed pro-American governments in order to curb potential expansion of Communism. Although Eisenhower favored such covert operations because they were relatively low-cost and attracted little attention, the coups in Iran and Guatemala proved rather transparent and caused international anger toward the United States.

JOHN FOSTER DULLES
Secretary of state under Eisenhower (and brother of Allen Dulles) who helped devise Eisenhower's **New Look** foreign policy. Dulles's policy emphasized **massive retaliation** with nuclear weapons. In particular, Dulles advocated the use of nuclear weapons against Ho Chi Minh's Communist forces in **Vietnam**.

DWIGHT D. EISENHOWER
A World War II hero and former supreme commander of **NATO** who became U.S. president in 1953 after easily defeating Democratic opponent **Adlai E. Stevenson**. Eisenhower expanded New Deal–era social welfare programs such as **Social Security** and passed the landmark **Federal Highway Act** to improve national transportation. However, he cut back funding to other domestic programs to halt what he called **"creeping socialism."** His **New Look** at foreign policy, meanwhile, emphasized nuclear weapons and the threat of massive retaliation against the Soviet Union in order to cut costs and deter the USSR from spreading Communism abroad. Eisenhower committed federal dollars to fighting Communists in **Vietnam**, resolved the **Suez crisis**, and authorized **CIA**-sponsored coups in Iran and Guatemala.

HO CHI MINH
The nationalist, Communist leader of the Viet Minh movement, which sought to liberate **Vietnam** from French colonial rule throughout the 1950s. After being rebuffed by the United States, Ho received aid from the USSR and won a major victory over

9

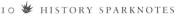

French forces at **Dien Bien Phu** in 1954. This French defeat forced the **Geneva Conference** of 1954, which split Vietnam into Communist-dominated North Vietnam and French-backed South Vietnam.

JOHN F. KENNEDY
The thirty-fifth U.S. president, who set out to expand social welfare spending with his **New Frontier** program. Kennedy was elected in 1960, defeating Republican **Richard M. Nixon**. Feeling that their hands were tied by Eisenhower's policy of "massive retaliation," Kennedy and members of his foreign policy staff devised the tactic of **"flexible response"** to contain Communism. Kennedy sent "military advisors" to support Ngo Dinh Diem's corrupt regime in **South Vietnam** and formed the **Alliance for Progress** to fight poverty and Communism in Latin America. He also backed the disastrous **Bay of Pigs invasion**, which ultimately led to the **Cuban missile crisis**. In 1963, after Kennedy had spent roughly 1,000 days in office, he was assassinated, and Vice President **Lyndon B. Johnson** took office.

NIKITA KHRUSHCHEV
The head of the Soviet Communist Party and leader of the USSR from 1958 until the early 1960s. Initially, many Americans hoped Khrushchev's rise to power would lead to a reduction in Cold War tensions. Khrushchev toured the United States in 1959 and visited personally with President Eisenhower at **Camp David**, Maryland. The **U-2 incident** and 1962 **Cuban missile crisis**, however, ended what little amity existed between the two nations and repolarized the Cold War. Party leaders, upset with Khrushchev for having backed down from the **Cuban missile crisis**, removed him from power in 1964.

DOUGLAS MACARTHUR
Five-star American general who commanded Allied forces in the Pacific during **World War II**. After the war, MacArthur led the American occupation in **Japan**, helped establish a democratic government there, and in large part rewrote the country's new constitution outlawing militarism. He later commanded United Nations forces in **Korea**, driving North Korean forces back north of the 38th parallel after making the brilliant **Inchon landing**. He ignored Chinese warnings not to approach the North Korean–Chinese border at the Yalu River, however, and was subsequently driven back down to the 38th parallel by more than a million Chinese troops. President **Harry S Truman** later rejected MacArthur's request to bomb North Korea

and China with nuclear weapons. MacArthur's public criticism of the president's decision prompted Truman to remove him from command in 1951.

JOSEPH MCCARTHY

Republican senator from Wisconsin who capitalized on Cold War fears of **Communism** in the early 1950s by accusing hundreds of government employees of being Communists and Soviet agents. Although McCarthy failed to offer any concrete evidence to prove these claims, many Americans fully supported him. He ruined his own reputation in 1954 after humiliating himself during the televised **Army-McCarthy hearings**. Disgraced, he received an official censure from the Senate and died an alcoholic in 1957.

GAMAL ABDEL NASSER

The nationalist, Communist-leaning president of **Egypt** who seized the British-controlled **Suez Canal** in 1956, after economic aid negotiations among Egypt, Great Britain, and the United States fell apart. Nasser's action precipitated the **Suez crisis**, in which Eisenhower uncharacteristically backed the Communist-leaning Nasser and cut off all oil exports to Great Britain and France.

RICHARD M. NIXON

Republican congressman from California who rose to national fame as a prominent member of the **House Un-American Activities Committee** in the late 1940s when he successfully prosecuted **Alger Hiss** for being a Communist. Nixon later served as vice president under **Dwight D. Eisenhower** from 1953 to 1961. He lost his own bid for the presidency against **John F. Kennedy** in 1960 but defeated his Democratic opponent eight years later and became president in 1969.

HARRY S TRUMAN

Vice president under **Franklin D. Roosevelt** who became president upon Roosevelt's death in April 1945 and successfully carried out the remainder of **World War II**. Truman was instrumental in creating a new international political and economic order after the war, helping to form the **United Nations**, **NATO**, the **World Bank**, and the **International Monetary Fund**. His **Marshall Plan** also helped Western Europe rebuild after the war and surpass its pre-war levels of industrial production. Determined not to let the Soviet Union spread Communism, Truman adopted the idea of **containment**, announcing his own **Truman Doctrine** in 1947.

His characterization of the Soviet Union as a force of "ungodly" evil helped shape the Cold War of the next four decades. He also led the nation into the **Korean War** but eventually fired General **Douglas MacArthur** for insubordination.

TERMS

ARMY-McCARTHY HEARINGS
Congressional hearings that took place in 1954 as a result of Wisconsin senator **Joseph McCarthy** accusing ranking U.S. Army officers of being **Communists** and Soviet spies. Tens of millions of Americans watched the televised courtroom proceedings as McCarthy publicly humiliated himself without offering a shred of evidence. The hearings earned McCarthy an official censure from his fellow senators, finished his political career, and effectively ended the **Red hunts**.

BAY OF PIGS INVASION
President **John F. Kennedy**'s failed plan to invade Cuba and topple revolutionary leader **Fidel Castro** with an army of CIA-trained Cuban exiles in 1961. Although Kennedy had originally intended to use the U.S. Air Force to help the exiled Cubans retake the island, he unexpectedly withdrew support shortly before the operation started. As a result, the invasion failed utterly, actually consolidated Castro's power, and pushed Cuba into signing a treaty with the Soviet Union.

BERLIN AIRLIFT
The dropping of thousands of tons of food and medical supplies to starving West Berliners after **Joseph Stalin** closed off all highway and railway access to the city in mid-1948. Stalin hoped to cut off British, French, and American access to the conquered German city, but President **Harry S Truman**, determined not to lose face or the city, ordered American military planes to drop provisions from the air. The blockade was foiled, and Stalin finally lifted it in 1949.

CONTAINMENT
A U.S. foreign policy doctrine that argued that the Soviet Union needed to be "contained" to prevent the spread of Communism throughout the world. First formulated by State Department analyst **George Kennan** during the Truman administration, it suggested that the United States needed to fight Communism abroad and promote democracy (or at least anti-Communist regimes) worldwide.

Policy makers tied it closely with the **domino theory**. Kennan's idea eventually developed into the single most important tenet of American foreign policy through the Cold War until the collapse of the Soviet Union in 1991.

CUBAN MISSILE CRISIS
The crisis that occurred when Cuban leader **Fidel Castro** sought economic and military assistance from the Soviet Union after the United States' failed 1961 **Bay of Pigs invasion**. The Soviet premier, **Nikita Khrushchev**, capitalized on the failed invasion, allied with Castro, and secured from Castro the right to place nuclear missiles in Cuba. Upon learning of the missiles, President **John F. Kennedy** ordered a **naval blockade** of the island in 1962 and demanded that Khrushchev remove them. Nuclear war seemed imminent until Khrushchev finally backed down, promising to remove the missiles if Kennedy ended the blockade. The United States complied and also agreed to remove from Turkey nuclear missiles aimed at the USSR. The Communist Party leadership in the USSR removed Khrushchev from power in 1964 for having backed down in the standoff.

DIEN BIEN PHU
A site in **Vietnam** where an important French outpost fell to **Ho Chi Minh**'s pro-Communist forces in 1954. After this defeat, an international conference in Geneva split Vietnam into two nations—North Vietnam and South Vietnam—with the dividing line at the **17th parallel**. Ho Chi Minh established a government in the city of **Hanoi** in North Vietnam, while U.S.-backed **Ngo Dinh Diem** took control of the South Vietnamese government in **Saigon**.

DOMINO THEORY
The belief that if the United States allowed one country to fall to Communism, then many more would follow suit, like a row of dominoes. Many foreign policy thinkers subscribed to this theory at the height of the Cold War, and this led the United States to support anti-Communist regimes throughout the world, whether or not they upheld democratic ideals. The domino theory also provided the primary rationale behind Lyndon Johnson's massive escalation of the conflict in **Vietnam** to full-scale war.

FLEXIBLE RESPONSE
A doctrine of **containment** that provided for a variety of military and political strategies that the president could use to stem the spread of Communism. The flexible response plan was developed by Defense

and State Department officials in the Kennedy administration who felt that Eisenhower's **"massive retaliation"** doctrine restricted the president's options too much.

HOUSE UN-AMERICAN ACTIVITIES COMMITTEE (HUAC)

A committee established in 1938 by the House of Representatives to investigate individual Americans or organizations who might be linked to the Nazis or the Ku Klux Klan. After World War II, as fear of the Soviet Union spread, HUAC was used to investigate those suspected of having ties to **Communism** or of being Soviet agents. Congressman **Richard M. Nixon** played a key role on the committee and used his power to prosecute many, including federal employee **Alger Hiss** in 1950.

MARSHALL PLAN

A plan devised by President **Harry S Truman** and Secretary of State **George C. Marshall** that committed over $10 billion to rebuilding **Western Europe** after World War II. Although the Soviet Union fiercely opposed the plan, Truman knew that rebuilding the region would provide stability and prevent another world war. The Marshall Plan was highly successful and enabled British, French, Italian, and German factories to exceed prewar production levels within just a few years.

MASSIVE RETALIATION

A primary component of **Dwight D. Eisenhower**'s **New Look** foreign policy that threatened massive **nuclear retaliation** against the Soviet Union for any Communist aggression abroad. Designed to save the U.S. government money on defense spending, this policy effectively tied Eisenhower's hands because it limited his options when addressing smaller crises, such as the 1956 **Hungarian Revolution**. Kennedy later dropped the threat of massive retaliation in favor of the doctrine of **"flexible response,"** which gave the president more options.

MONTGOMERY G.I. BILL

A bill passed in 1944 that provided federal grants for **education** to returning World War II **veterans**. Also known as the **Servicemen's Readjustment Act**, the bill also awarded federal **loans** to vets to purchase new homes, farms, and businesses. Millions of veterans took advantage of these grants and loans to go back to school and purchase new suburban homes, making the act one of the most significant pieces of postwar legislation.

NATIONAL SECURITY ACT
An act passed in 1947 that reorganized the U.S. military and espionage services in order to better meet the Soviet threat. The act placed the armed forces under the new **secretary of defense** and **Joint Chiefs of Staff** and also created the **Central Intelligence Agency** and the **National Security Council** to advise the president.

NATIONAL SECURITY COUNCIL MEMORANDUM 68 (NSC-68)
A classified 1950 proposal that the United States quadruple defense and military spending in order to counter the Soviet threat. NSC-68 set a precedent for increasing defense spending throughout the Cold War, especially after North Korean forces attacked South Korea in June 1950.

NEW FRONTIER
Kennedy's collective bundle of domestic policies, which called for increased **social welfare spending** to tackle the growing poverty rate. Opposition in Congress from Republicans and southern Democrats, however, blocked the passage of most New Frontier legislation.

NORTH ATLANTIC TREATY ORGANIZATION (NATO)
An organization formed in 1949 that bound the United States, Canada, most of Western Europe, and later Greece and Turkey together in a mutual pact of defense against the USSR and Eastern bloc countries. The treaty had the additional effect of permanently tying American interests to political and economic stability in Europe.

RED HUNTS
The wrongful persecutions of thousands of Americans for being Communists or Soviet spies that took place in the 1940s and 1950s and were led by the **Loyalty Review Board** and the **House Un-American Activities Committee**. Congressman **Richard Nixon**, Senator **Joseph McCarthy**, and others led these Communist "witch hunts," often without any shred of evidence. Liberal playwright **Arthur Miller**, himself among the accused Communists, criticized the Red hunts and McCarthyism in his critically acclaimed play *The Crucible*, which dealt with the Salem witch trials in seventeenth-century New England.

SPACE RACE

The Cold War competition between the United States and the Soviet Union for primacy in the exploration of outer space. The space race was prompted by the USSR's launch of the first orbiting space satellite, *Sputnik I*, in 1957. The *Sputnik* launch prompted President Eisenhower to form **NASA** and Kennedy to push for a **lunar landing** by the end of the 1960s.

SPUTNIK I AND SPUTNIK II

The first orbiting space satellites, launched by the Soviet Union beginning in 1957. The launch of these satellites astonished the world and scared many Americans into believing that the USSR had the capability to attack the United States with long-range nuclear missiles. President Eisenhower responded by forming the **National Aeronautics and Space Administration (NASA)** to coordinate American endeavors to explore space. Congress also passed the **National Defense Education Act**, which provided more federal dollars for science and foreign language instruction in public schools. American and Soviet competition to explore space quickly became known as the **space race**.

SUEZ CRISIS

The crisis that erupted after Egypt's nationalization of the British-controlled **Suez Canal**, which took place in 1956 after negotiations over international aid among the United States, Great Britain, and Egypt collapsed. Egyptian president **Gamal Abdel Nasser** nationalized the canal, which links the Red Sea and the Mediterranean Sea. Although Eisenhower protested the move, he also condemned the joint British, French, and Israeli invasion of Egypt to retake the canal. The three nations eventually halted their attack and withdrew, under heavy diplomatic and economic pressure from the United States.

TRUMAN DOCTRINE

A doctrine articulated by President **Harry S Truman** that pledged American support for all "free peoples" fighting Communist aggression from foreign or domestic sources. Truman announced the doctrine in 1947, then convinced Congress to grant Greece and Turkey $400 million to help fight pro-Soviet insurgents. Besides committing the United States to the policy of containment, the language of the Truman Doctrine itself help characterize the Cold War as a conflict between good and evil.

U-2 INCIDENT

The crisis that arose after the USSR shot down an American **U-2** spy plane flying over the USSR on a reconnaissance mission in 1960. President **Dwight D. Eisenhower** initially denied that the incident occurred until Soviet premier **Nikita Khrushchev** presented the captured American pilot. The president's refusal to apologize or halt future spy missions caused the collapse of a joint summit among Great Britain, France, the United States, and the USSR in May 1960.

WARSAW PACT

A pact signed by the USSR and Eastern European countries under Soviet influence in 1955. By signing the pact, they pledged mutual defense in response to the formation of **NATO**.

KEY PEOPLE & TERMS

Summary & Analysis

The Postwar World: 1945–1949

Key People

Harry S Truman 33rd U.S. president; successfully carried out end of World War II after FDR's death; helped create new postwar political and economic world order

Joseph Stalin Soviet premier; opposed reindustrialization of Germany outlined in the Marshall Plan; ordered Berlin blockade

Douglas MacArthur U.S. Army general; commanded Allied forces in the Pacific during World War II and subsequently led U.S. occupation of Japan

Postwar Predicaments

As **World War II** combat operations ceased in Europe and the war drew rapidly to a close in the Pacific, the United States and its new president, **Harry S Truman**, faced many new challenges. War criminals had to be punished, Europe and Japan had to be rebuilt, the global economy had to be restructured, and the United States had to ensure that another world war would not erupt.

At first, Truman seemed unfit to solve these problems. The product of a Missouri political machine, he had minimal experience with international affairs, having served only as senator and then just months as Franklin D. Roosevelt's fourth-term vice president. Despite his relative inexperience, however, Truman quickly acclimated to his new position and proved capable of tackling these postwar problems.

The Bretton Woods Conference

The process of rebuilding Europe began almost a year before Truman became president, when the United States invited Allied delegates to discuss the postwar world in **Bretton Woods**, New Hampshire, in July 1944. At the conclusion of the conference, delegates had created two major world financial institutions: the **World**

Bank, to help stimulate development in third world countries, and the **International Monetary Fund (IMF)**, to regulate exchange rates.

THE UNITED NATIONS

Stalin's representatives were, however, involved in the formation of the **United Nations**, which was intended to promote international security and prevent future global conflicts. Meeting in April 1945, just days after Franklin D. Roosevelt's death and Truman's succession to the presidency, delegates drafted the organization's founding charter, which closely resembled the charter of the failed **League of Nations** after World War I. Because World War II had proved that the United States could no longer remain isolated from world affairs, the new charter passed easily through the Senate ratification process that summer. According to the charter, the United States, Great Britain, France, China, and the USSR each would have a permanent seat and veto power on the governing **Security Council**.

ISRAEL

One of the first tasks for the United Nations was the creation of the Jewish nation of **Israel**. Carved out of British **Palestine** along the eastern Mediterranean, this new state became the home for millions of displaced Jews who had survived centuries of persecution. Hoping to keep the Soviet Union out of Israel, win Jewish-American votes, and capitalize on the American public's postwar sympathy for the Jewish people, Truman ignored his foreign policy advisors and officially recognized Israel in 1948. Although the decision gave the United States a strategic foothold in the Middle East, it also ruined relations with the Arab countries in the region and Muslim nations around the world.

REBUILDING JAPAN

The process of rebuilding **Japan** began almost as soon as the war ended. The commander of the Allied forces in the Pacific, U.S. Army general **Douglas MacArthur**, spearheaded the democratization and reconstruction process—a daunting task considering the widespread devastation throughout Japan. MacArthur rounded up ranking officers in the Japanese military leadership and tried them as war criminals in the **Tokyo trials**. The Japanese, for their part, accepted defeat and worked hard to rebuild their country under U.S. guidelines.

　　Within a year, MacArthur and the Japanese drafted a new democratic constitution, and the United States pledged military protec-

SUMMARY & ANALYSIS

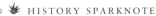

tion in exchange for a promise that Japan would not rearm. The new constitution and reforms allowed Japan to recover quickly from the war and eventually boast one of the largest economies in the world.

Rebuilding Germany

Rebuilding **Germany** proved to be a far more difficult task. At the time of the German surrender in 1945, British, French, American, and Soviet troops occupied different regions of the country. Although located deep within the Soviet-occupied zone in the east, the German capital city of **Berlin** also contained troops from each of the other three countries, occupying different districts.

Although all four nations agreed that it was necessary to punish the Nazi leadership for war crimes at the **Nuremberg trials**, none of the powers wanted to relinquish control of its occupied territory. It quickly became clear that the problem of control in Germany would simply remain unresolved. The British, French, and American occupation zones eventually merged into the independent **West Germany** in 1949, while the Soviet half ultimately became **East Germany**. All four powers, however, continued to occupy Berlin jointly—likewise splitting it into West Berlin and East Berlin—until Germany was finally reunified in 1990.

The Marshall Plan

The Soviet Union in particular wanted to exact revenge on Germany by dismantling its factories and demanding outrageous **war reparations**. Truman realized, however, that punitive action would only destabilize Germany further, just as it had after the signing of the unforgiving **Treaty of Versailles** that had ended World War I.

In 1947, Truman's secretary of state, **George C. Marshall**, pledged that the United States would grant more than $10 billion to help rebuild Europe if the European nations themselves worked together to help meet this end. Great Britain, France, Italy, and Germany complied and came together to lead postwar Europe—an early precursor to the **European Community** and **European Union** that would come later. The **Marshall Plan**, as it came to be known, stabilized Western Europe financially and prevented economic collapse. Within ten years, European factories had exceeded prewar production levels, boosting the standard of living and ensuring that Communism would not take root.

THE IRON CURTAIN

Although the United States and the Marshall Plan controlled West Germany's fate, Stalin dictated policy in occupied East Germany. Determined to build a buffer between Germany and Moscow, the Soviet **Red Army** established Communist governments in the eastern capitals it occupied at the end of the war. As a result, the USSR created an **"iron curtain"** that effectively separated East Germany, Poland, Hungary, Czechoslovakia, Yugoslavia, Ukraine, Belarus, Romania, Bulgaria, Latvia, Estonia, and Lithuania from the West.

THE BERLIN CRISIS AND AIRLIFT

In 1948, Stalin attempted to drive British, French, and American forces out of Berlin by cutting off all highway and railway access to the Western-controlled portion of the city. Truman refused to withdraw U.S. troops; control of Berlin had become such an enormous symbol in the U.S.-Soviet standoff that Truman could not afford the political cost of caving under Stalin's threats. Instead, he ordered American airplanes to drop millions of tons of food and medical supplies to West Berlin's residents in 1948 and 1949. Americans and Europeans hailed the **Berlin airlift** as a major victory over the Soviet Union. Stalin eventually ended the **Berlin crisis** when he reopened the roads and railways in 1949.

THE START OF THE COLD WAR:
1947–1952

EVENTS

1938	House Un-American Activities Committee created
1947	Doctrine of containment emerges Truman articulates Truman Doctrine Congress passes National Security Act
1948	Alger Hiss accused of being a Soviet operative Truman is reelected
1949	NATO is formed China falls to Communist forces
1950	Congress passes McCarran Internal Security Bill
1951	Julius and Ethel Rosenberg convicted of espionage
1952	United States develops first hydrogen bomb

KEY PEOPLE

Harry S Truman 33rd U.S. president; announced Truman Doctrine in 1947, which shaped U.S. foreign policy for four decades

Thomas E. Dewey New York governor who ran unsuccessfully on the Republican Party ticket against Truman in 1948

George F. Kennan State Department analyst who developed containment doctrine in 1947, arguing that Communism and the USSR could not be allowed to spread; this doctrine became the basis of U.S. foreign policy strategy during the Cold War

Richard M. Nixon Republican congressman and prominent member of HUAC in the late 1940s; successfully prosecuted Alger Hiss for being a Communist

Alger Hiss Former federal employee prosecuted by HUAC in 1948–1950 for being a Communist and Soviet spy

Julius and Ethel Rosenberg Married couple convicted of espionage in 1951 after being wrongfully convicted of selling nuclear secrets to the USSR; executed in 1953

Chiang Kai-shek Leader of China's Nationalist government when Communist forces drove it out of mainland China in 1949

Mao Zedong Leader of Communist revolutionaries who brought down China's Nationalist government in 1949; became ruler of People's Republic of China as leader of Chinese Communist Party

CONTAINMENT

In 1947, State Department analyst **George F. Kennan** penned a highly influential essay on the Soviet Union that transformed fear of the USSR into a cohesive foreign policy. Arguing that insecure Russians had always had the desire to expand and acquire territory, Kennan wrote that the Soviet Union would take every opportunity to spread Communism into every possible "nook and cranny" around the globe, either by conquering neighboring countries or by subtly supporting Communist revolutionaries in politically unstable countries. Kennan also wrote, however, that the United States could prevent the global domination of Communism with a strategy of **"containment."** He suggested maintaining the status quo by thwarting Communist aggression abroad.

Kennan's containment doctrine rapidly became the root of the dominant U.S. strategy for fighting Communism throughout the Cold War. Different presidents interpreted the doctrine differently and/or employed different tactics to accomplish their goals, but the overall strategy for keeping Communism in check remained the same until the Cold War ended in the early 1990s.

THE TRUMAN DOCTRINE

Truman quickly latched onto the doctrine of containment and modified it with his own **Truman Doctrine**. In a special address to Congress in March 1947, Truman announced that the United States would support foreign governments resisting "armed minorities" or "outside pressures"—that is, Communist revolutionaries or the Soviet Union. He then convinced Congress to appropriate $400 million to prevent the fall of Greece and Turkey to Communist insurgents.

Critics, both at the time and looking back in retrospect, have charged that Truman's adoption of the containment doctrine, coupled with his own Truman Doctrine, accelerated the Cold War by polarizing the United States and the USSR unnecessarily. Many have claimed that the United States might have avoided fifty years of competition and mutual distrust had Truman sought a diplomatic solution instead.

Defendants of Truman's policy, however, have claimed that the Soviet Union had already begun the Cold War by thwarting Allied attempts to reunite and stabilize Germany. Truman, they have argued, merely met the existing Soviet challenge. Other supporters believed that Truman used polarizing language in order to prevent U.S. isolationists from abandoning the cause in Europe. Whatever his motivations, Truman's adoption of the containment doctrine and his characterization of the Communist threat shaped American foreign policy for the subsequent four decades.

THE NATIONAL SECURITY ACT

The possibility of a war with the Soviet Union prompted Congress, Truman, and the military leadership to drastically reorganize the intelligence-gathering services and armed forces. In 1947, Congress passed the landmark **National Security Act**, which placed the military under the new cabinet-level **secretary of defense**. Civilians would be chosen to serve in the post of secretary of defense and as the secretaries of the individual military branches, while the highest-ranking officers in the armed forces would form the new **Joint Chiefs of Staff** to coordinate military efforts. The National Security Act also created the civilian position of **national security advisor** to advise the president and direct the new **National Security Council**. The new **Central Intelligence Agency** became the primary espionage and intelligence-gathering service.

THE ELECTION OF 1948

Even though he had initially complained about his new responsibilities as president after Roosevelt's death in 1945, Truman decided to run for reelection as the prospect of another world war loomed. Party leaders nominated him only halfheartedly after World War II hero Dwight D. Eisenhower refused to run on the Democratic ticket. Conservative southern Democrats in particular disliked Truman's New Deal–esque commitment to labor, civil rights, reform, and social welfare spending. When Truman received the formal party nomination, southern Democrats split from the party and nominated their own candidate, Governor **Strom Thurmond** of South Carolina. Progressive Democrats also nominated former vice president **Henry Wallace** on a pro-peace platform.

The Republicans, meanwhile, nominated New York governor **Thomas E. Dewey**. Most Democrats and even Truman himself believed victory to be impossible. On election night, the *Chicago Tribune* printed an early version of the election returns, proclaiming a Dewey win with the infamous headline "Dewey Defeats Truman." As it turned out, however, Truman received more than two million more popular votes than his nearest challenger, Dewey, and 303 electoral votes. He owed his victory in part to his adoption of the policy of containment but mostly to his commitment to expand Social Security and provide increased social welfare spending as part of his proposed **Fair Deal** program. Continued Republican and southern Democrat opposition in Congress, though, blocked the majority of Fair Deal legislation during Truman's second term.

NATO AND THE WARSAW PACT

With the mandate from the election, Truman pushed ahead with his programs to defend Western Europe from possible attack. In 1949, the United States joined Great Britain, France, Italy, Canada, the Netherlands, Luxembourg, Belgium, Denmark, Norway, Iceland, and Portugal in forming a military alliance called the **North Atlantic**

Treaty Organization (NATO). The NATO charter pledged that an attack on one of the member nations constituted an attack on all of the members. Greece and Turkey signed the treaty in 1952, followed by West Germany in 1955.

Perhaps the greatest significance of NATO was the fact that it committed the United States to Western Europe and prevented U.S. conservatives in the future from isolating the United States from the world as they had after World War I. Outraged and threatened, the USSR and the Soviet bloc countries it dominated in Eastern Europe made similar pledges of mutual defense.

THE FALL OF CHINA

Meanwhile, events unfolding in **China** had enormous repercussions on the United States and ultimately on the Cold War itself. For decades, the Nationalist government of **Chiang Kai-shek** (sometimes written as Jiang Jieshi) had been fighting a long civil war against Communist rebels led by **Mao Zedong** (or Mao Tse-tung). The U.S. government under Roosevelt and Truman had backed the Nationalists with money and small arms shipments but overall had little influence on the war. Mao's revolutionaries, however, finally managed to defeat government forces in 1949 and took control of mainland China.

While Chiang and his supporters fled to the island of Taiwan, Communist Party chairman Mao became the head of the new **People's Republic of China (PRC).** The so-called **fall of China** was a crushing blow for the United States, primarily because it suddenly put more than a quarter of the world's population under Communist control. Moreover, previous U.S. support for Chiang Kai-shek also meant that the PRC would not look favorably upon the United States.

THE ARMS RACE

Also in 1949, Truman announced that the Soviet Union had successfully tested its first **atomic bomb,** sooner than American scientists had predicted. Even though it would have been difficult for the USSR to actually drop a nuclear bomb on U.S. soil—nuclear missiles would not be invented for another decade—the Soviets' discovery cost Truman the diplomatic upper hand. Whereas the United States had lorded its nuclear superiority over the Soviets' heads in the past, it could no longer do so.

To regain the upper hand, Truman poured federal dollars into the 1952 development of the **hydrogen bomb,** an even more devastating weapon than the original atomic bomb. Its developers feared this weapon would become a tool for genocide. The Soviet Union responded in kind with its own H-bomb the following year, ratcheting the stakes even higher. The United States and the USSR continued competing against each other with the development of greater and more destructive weapons in an **arms race** that lasted until the end of the Cold War.

THE SECOND RED SCARE

The fall of China, the Soviets' development of nuclear weapons, and the crises in Europe all contributed to Americans' growing fear of Communism at home. Remembering the Bolshevik revolutionaries' cry for the global destruction of capitalism, frightened Americans began hunting for Communist revolutionaries within the United States and elsewhere. President Truman had already created the **Loyalty Review Board** in 1947 to investigate all federal departments, and the State Department in particular, to uncover any hidden Soviet agents working to overthrow the government. The board went into overdrive at the end of the decade, and thousands of innocent individuals were wrongfully accused and persecuted as a result.

RED HUNTS

As a member of the **House Un-American Activities Committee (HUAC)**, Congressman **Richard M. Nixon** of California helped spearhead the search for Communists in the government. In 1948, he prosecuted former federal employee and accused Communist **Alger Hiss** in one of the most dramatic cases of the decade. Hiss's trial dragged on for two more years and ended with a five-year prison sentence for perjury. Prosecutors also charged husband and wife **Julius and Ethel Rosenberg** with having given American nuclear secrets to Soviet agents—an allegation that, though debated for decades after the trial, was corroborated by Soviet intelligence documents released in the 1990s. The Rosenbergs were convicted in 1951 and sent to the electric chair in 1953, becoming the first American civilians ever executed for espionage.

Although the Red hunts resulted in the capture of legitimate spies such as the Rosenbergs, Truman began to realize by the end of his presidency that the fear of Communism had caused widespread and undue panic. He tried to tame the Red-hunters in 1950 when he vetoed the **McCarran Internal Security Bill**, which he believed would give the U.S. president too much power to subvert civil liberties. Republicans in Congress, however, overrode Truman's veto and passed the bill into law later that year.

THE KOREAN WAR: 1950–1953

EVENTS

1950	Korean War begins U.S. forces land at Inchon MacArthur retakes South Korea Chinese troops force MacArthur back to Seoul
1951	Truman fires MacArthur
1952	Dwight D. Eisenhower is elected president
1953	Korean War ends with signing of armistice

KEY PEOPLE

Harry S Truman 33rd U.S. president; was commander in chief during most of Korean War
Dean Acheson Secretary of state during Truman's second term; announced in 1950 that
    Korea was outside the U.S. defense perimeter
Douglas MacArthur U.S. general and commander of United Nations forces who drove
    North Korean forces back past the 38th parallel after making Inchon landing
Dwight D. Eisenhower 34th U.S. president; elected in 1952 after serving as general in
    World War II and as supreme commander of NATO; secured cease-fire in Korea

NORTH AND SOUTH KOREA

With Hitler and Mussolini defeated in Europe in 1945, the United
States and Soviet Union turned to fighting Japan later in the year.
After Japanese forces surrendered to General **Douglas MacArthur**,
the United States and the USSR shared control of the neighboring
Korean Peninsula, which had been under Japanese control since the
turn of the century. They divided Korea at the **38th parallel**, with the
Soviet Union taking control in the north and the United States in the
south. Both sides also armed the Koreans and erected new governments friendly to each respective superpower.

THE START OF THE KOREAN WAR

It seemed that Korea might become a flash point in the Cold War,
but then Truman's secretary of state, **Dean Acheson**, effectively
announced in 1950 that the United States had no interest in Korea
because it had no geopolitical significance. The Soviet Union, however, may have interpreted Acheson's remarks as giving the USSR
carte blanche regarding Korea and therefore allowed the North
Korean Communist government in Pyongyang to invade South
Korea in June 1950, with some Soviet support. Outnumbered and
outgunned, the South Korean forces retreated to the city of **Pusan** on
the peninsula's southern shore. Truman watched, stunned, as the
North Korean forces captured almost the entire peninsula within
the span of a few months. He capitalized on the Soviet Union's

absence in the United Nations Security Council, however, to convince the other members that North Korea had been the sole aggressor. After a vote of unanimous approval, the Security Council asked all member nations to help restore peace.

NSC-68

Both conservative and liberal foreign policy makers in the United States viewed the North Korean invasion as evidence that the Soviet Union did in fact hope to spread Communism and as a threat to American efforts to rebuild and democratize Japan. The invasion thus made George F. Kennan's theories about **containment** all the more pertinent: Truman worried that if the United States failed to act, the Soviet Union would continue to expand and threaten democracy.

In order to check this feared expansion, Truman's new National Security Council submitted a classified document known simply as **National Security Council Memorandum 68 (NSC-68)**, which suggested that Truman quadruple military spending for purposes of containment. The president readily consented and asked Congress for more funds and more men. Within a few years, the U.S. armed forces boasted more than 3 million men, and the United States was spending roughly 15 percent of its gross national product on the military.

THE INCHON LANDING

Truman made sure that General MacArthur, who had been an effective in overseeing occupied postwar Japan, was made commander of the UN forces sent to Korea. Truman then ordered MacArthur to pull U.S. troops out of Japan and retake South Korea below the 38th parallel.

In September 1950, MacArthur and his troops flanked the North Koreans by making an amphibious landing at Inchon, near Seoul. The surprise **Inchon landing** allowed U.S. forces to enter the peninsula quickly, without having to break through the enormous forces surrounding Pusan. Caught entirely off guard, the North Korean forces panicked and fled north, well past the 38th parallel. Truman ordered MacArthur to cross the parallel and pursue the North Koreans.

DISASTER AT THE YALU RIVER

MacArthur's crossing of the 38th parallel troubled the Soviet Union and Communist China, especially considering that Truman had entered the war vowing to restore peace and the status quo—not to conquer the entire peninsula. China therefore warned the United States not to approach the Chinese–North Korean border at the **Yalu River**. However, MacArthur ignored the warning and pursued the North Koreans farther up the peninsula. Interpreting this move as an act of war, the Chinese sent hundreds of thousands of soldiers across the Yalu to meet MacArthur's men in North Korea. Overwhelmed, MacArthur and his forces retreated back to the 38th parallel.

MacArthur's Dismissal

Stalemated once again at the 38th parallel, MacArthur pressured Truman to drop nuclear bombs on mainland China. Doing so, MacArthur reasoned, would not only allow his forces to take the entire Korean Peninsula but would also topple the Communist regime in Beijing. Truman and U.S. military officials, however, knew they lacked the resources to fight a war with China, defend Western Europe, contain the Soviet Union, occupy Japan, and hold Korea at the same time. They also wanted to keep the war limited and knew that the deployment of nuclear weapons would bring the Soviet Union into what could quickly devolve into World War III. MacArthur rebuffed these arguments and instead tried to turn the American people against Truman by criticizing him in public. Truman removed MacArthur from command in April 1951, for insubordination.

The Election of 1952

Even though MacArthur had disobeyed orders and publicly rebuked the commander-in-chief, blame fell on Truman for "losing" Korea to the Communists. Since Truman had little chance of being reelected, Democrats instead nominated Illinois governor **Adlai E. Stevenson** for the presidency in 1952. Republicans, meanwhile, nominated former World War II general and NATO supreme commander **Dwight D. Eisenhower** for president, with former Red-hunter **Richard M. Nixon** as his running mate. Eisenhower's status as a war hero and Nixon's reputation for being tough on Communists gave the Republicans an easy victory. They won the popular vote by a 7 million-vote margin and also won a landslide in the electoral college, with 442 electoral votes to Stevenson's 89.

The End of the Korean War

By the time Eisenhower took the oath of office in 1953, American soldiers had been entrenched in Korea for nearly three years. In the time since MacArthur's final retreat to the 38th parallel, thousands more Americans had died without any territorial loss or gain. Eisenhower eventually brought about an **armistice** with North Korea, in part by making it known that he, unlike Truman, would consider the use of nuclear weapons in Korea. Despite the armistice, however, the border between North and South Korea has remained one of the most heavily fortified Cold War "hot spots" in the world for more than fifty years.

POSTWAR PROSPERITY AT HOME:
1945–1960

POSTWAR FINANCIAL FEARS

As World War II drew to a close, many Americans worried about the domestic economy. Although the war had spurred employment and production and had pulled the nation out of the Great Depression, the war economy couldn't last forever. Moreover, millions of veterans would soon return home in search of jobs that might not be there anymore. As inflation soared, many feared that the immediate postwar **recession** of 1946 and 1947 heralded the return of the Great Depression.

Truman and Congress took steps to address the economic downturn. In 1946, for instance, Congress passed the **Employment Act**, which created the **Council of Economic Advisors** to help Truman maximize national employment.

THE TAFT-HARTLEY ACT

During the recession, literally millions of industrial laborers went on strike to protest inadequate wages. Truman continued to support the labor unions as he had during the war, but conservatives feared that halting industrial production would severely cripple the economy. To remedy this problem, Republicans in Congress passed the **Taft-Hartley Act** in 1947, over Truman's veto, to restrict the influence of unions. The act outlawed all-union workplaces, made unions liable for damages incurred during interunion disputes, and required labor organizers to denounce Communism and take oaths of loyalty.

THE MONTGOMERY G.I. BILL

Perhaps the most important measure taken in combating the recession was the **Montgomery G.I. Bill**, which Congress had passed in 1944 to help the 15 million returning U.S. veterans reenter the job market. Also known as the **Servicemen's Readjustment Act** and the

G.I. Bill of Rights, the G.I. Bill gave government grants to any veteran who wished to return to school. Neither Truman nor Congress predicted that more than half of returning veterans would take advantage of approximately $15 billion in federal grants to attend vocational schools, colleges, and universities. The G.I. Bill also set aside an equal amount of money to provide veterans with loans for new homes, farms, and businesses.

Historians have since hailed the Montgomery G.I. Bill as the most significant law passed to address the concerns of the postwar years. It reduced fierce competition for jobs after the war and boosted the economy by helping millions of workers acquire new skills. Many have claimed that the economic boom in the 1950s would never have happened at all without the G.I. Bill.

THE POSTWAR BOOM

Indeed, the U.S. economy recovered quickly from the brief recession of 1946–1947 and then veritably exploded, making Americans the wealthiest people in the world. For approximately twenty years, the U.S. economic surge seemed unstoppable. Within just a few years, almost two-thirds of American families achieved middle-class status. **Gross national product (GNP)** more than doubled during the 1950s and then doubled again in the 1960s. By 1960, most American families had a car, a TV, and a refrigerator and owned their own home—an amazing achievement given that fewer than half of Americans had any of these luxuries just thirty years earlier.

FOUNDATIONS OF PROSPERITY

Wartime **industrial production** and unprecedented **defense spending** during the 1950s and 1960s fueled the economic boom. Whereas the manufacturing infrastructures in Great Britain, France, and Germany had been destroyed by invasion and bombing, American industries had remained completely untouched and therefore benefited greatly from the war. Federal dollars—roughly half of the congressional budget in the 1950s and 1960s—later kept these war factories running throughout the Cold War. Low oil prices, along with Eisenhower's investment in transportation infrastructure with the **Federal Highway Act** in 1956, also boosted the nation's overall economic strength. Improvements in education thanks to the G.I. Bill also improved workers' productivity.

WHITE-COLLAR WORKERS

The shift in the economic base away from agriculture and manufacturing and toward **"white-collar" jobs** also contributed significantly to the postwar boom. By 1960, the family homestead that had once dominated American economic life even up to the turn of the twentieth century had all but disappeared. Instead, corporate "agribusinesses" had take over agricultural production by using machinery that was more efficient than farmhands. Similarly, white-collar workers rapidly began to outnumber "blue-collar" manual laborers for the first time in U.S. history. This transformation contributed to the **decline of labor unions** in the latter half of the twentieth century.

SCIENTIFIC PROGRESS

New scientific discoveries and technological developments also spurred the economic boom. Federal grants encouraged companies to invest in **research and development** to make production more efficient. Government money also subsidized the development of **commercial airlines**, which contributed significantly to the economy by transporting goods and people across the country within hours rather than days or weeks. The development of the **transistor** rapidly transformed the electronics industry and resulted in the formation of new technology corporations. Nutrition and public health also improved during these years. **Jonas Salk**'s development of the **polio vaccine** in 1952, for example, effectively eliminated a disease that had killed and crippled hundreds of thousands of Americans in the past, including former president Franklin D. Roosevelt.

MIGRATION AND POPULATION BOOM

Meanwhile, the U.S. population redistributed itself geographically and grew dramatically during the postwar years. Improvements in transportation mobilized Americans: whereas the railroads of the Gilded Age had opened the West, interstates and airplanes developed it. During the 1950s and 1960s, millions of Americans left the East for the West, South, and Midwest. Federal grants to these regions contributed to their development. As a result, populations doubled, tripled, and even quadrupled in California, Arizona, New Mexico, Texas, Florida, and other so-called **Sun Belt** states. By the early 1960s, California had become the most populous state in the Union. On top of this migration, the postwar **"baby boom"** between 1945 and 1957 increased the U.S. population rapidly, as young Americans took advantage of the postwar peace and their increased wealth to start new families and have children.

THE AFRICAN-AMERICAN MIGRATION

Blacks, meanwhile, continued to move in large numbers from the South to northern and northeastern cities—a move that has become known as the **African-American migration**. The Great Depression, the invention of the mechanical cotton picker in the 1940s, World War II, and the prospect of jobs in northern cities prompted more than a million blacks to leave the South. This migration improved blacks' overall economic status and ultimately helped make the **civil rights movement** possible.

THE GROWTH OF THE SUBURBS

As blacks moved to the cities, many whites moved out of urban areas and into the suburbs. This pattern came to be known as **"white flight."** New housing developments, higher incomes, G.I. Bill loans to veterans, and the construction of interstates all contributed to the massive growth of American **suburbia** during the 1950s. The rapid development of shopping malls and fast-food restaurants matched the growth of the suburbs. Amusement parks, credit cards, and the availability of cheaper consumer goods followed as well, and Americans quickly developed the world's foremost **consumer culture**.

THE ENTERTAINMENT EXPLOSION

Consumerism, in turn, prompted the **entertainment industry** to invent new ways for Americans to amuse themselves. By the mid-1960s, 90 percent of American families owned televisions, and more and more spent the bulk of their free time watching TV. **Sitcoms**, such as *Leave It to Beaver*, *Ozzie and Harriet*, and *I Love Lucy*, were particularly popular because they idealized the new American consumer lifestyle.

The new musical genre of **rock and roll** gained popularity among American youth. Sexually charged songs by artists such as Elvis Presley, Buddy Holly, Chubby Checker, and, later, the Beatles dominated the airwaves and transformed popular music. At the same time, many new American writers in the 1950s, including members of the **Beat Generation**, such as poet Allen Ginsberg and author Jack Kerouac, challenged the new consumerist conformity that pervaded American life.

EISENHOWER AT HOME: 1952–1959

EVENTS

1952	Dwight D. Eisenhower is elected president
1954	Army-McCarthy hearings held Supreme Court issues *Brown v. Board of Education* of Topeka, Kansas, ruling
1955	AFL-CIO forms
1956	Congress passes Federal Highway Act
1957	Congress passes Civil Rights Act of 1957 Little Rock crisis erupts
1959	Congress passes Landrum-Griffin Act

KEY PEOPLE

Dwight D. Eisenhower 34th U.S. president; expanded New Deal–era social welfare programs and passed Federal Highway Act but cut back funding to other domestic programs in order to halt "creeping socialism"

Joseph McCarthy Republican senator from Wisconsin who led Communist witch hunts in the early 1950s; humiliated himself during televised Army-McCarthy hearings by making outlandish accusations with no evidence; was censured by the Senate

SUMMARY & ANALYSIS

CREEPING SOCIALISM

Eisenhower entered the White House in 1953 determined to roll back Franklin D. Roosevelt's New Deal liberalism, which he derided as **"creeping socialism."** A Republican, Eisenhower wanted to reduce the size and influence of the federal government, give more power to state governments, and allow corporate profits to boost the national economy unfettered. Less government influence, he reasoned, would put America back on track. He appointed prominent businessmen to top cabinet posts in an effort to make the executive branch more efficient. Most Americans praised his hands-off approach to government after twenty years of heavy social engineering under Roosevelt and Truman.

CONTINUING THE NEW DEAL

Eisenhower's desire to halt "creeping socialism" did not, however, mean dismantling the new social welfare programs previously put into place. Eisenhower proved to be a big proponent of programs and policies designed to help those at the bottom rung of the economic ladder, who needed help the most. He created the cabinet-level **Department of Health, Education, and Welfare** and allowed the government to continue to subsidize farmers so that the price of farm products remained high. Eisenhower expanded **Social Security** in order to benefit more Americans, including the elderly and unemployed, and also dumped more federal dollars into the **Federal Housing Administration** to help Americans purchase new homes.

THE FEDERAL HIGHWAY ACT

Most important, Eisenhower endorsed the **Federal Highway Act** in 1956, calling for the construction of a network of **interstate highways,** which would improve national transportation. In fewer than twenty years, this highway construction became the largest public works project in U.S. history and cost more than $25 billion. New taxes on gasoline, oil, and trucks helped pay for this massive endeavor. The new interstates had an enormous impact on the growth of the suburbs and prosperity but also severely crippled the development of public transportation systems.

THE AFL-CIO

Afraid that a Republican in the White House would mean the end of **organized labor**, which had flourished under the Democrats and during World War II, the heads of the rival **American Federation of Labor (AFL)** and the **Congress of Industrial Organizations (CIO)** labor unions merged in 1955 to create the **AFL-CIO.** This new superunion joined between 10 and 15 million workers under a single umbrella organization and helped millions of families achieve unprecedented prosperity. Never again have so many American laborers been organized in one body.

Scandal after scandal rocked the organization in the 1960s and 1970s, including the expulsion of the **Teamsters Union** from the AFL-CIO in 1957 for having ties to organized crime. The media attention tarnished organized labor in the public eye and convinced millions to leave the union. Congress eventually passed the 1959 **Landrum-Griffin Act** in the wake of these scandals to limit labor unions' rights.

IKE ON CIVIL RIGHTS

Eisenhower privately opposed the **civil rights movement** and remained relatively silent as the movement began to gain momentum during his presidency. He made no comment after the Supreme Court ruled unanimously in *Brown v. Board of Education of Topeka, Kansas*, that "separate but equal" public facilities for blacks and whites were unconstitutional. He signed the **Civil Rights Act of 1957**, but only reluctantly and only after assuring southern legislators that the new law would have little real impact.

Eisenhower did, however, exert federal authority that same year when Arkansas governor **Orval Faubus** defied a federal court order and mobilized National Guard units to prevent nine black students from entering Central High School in Little Rock. Eisenhower resolved the **Little Rock crisis** by placing the National Guard under federal control and sending more than 1,000 U.S. Army soldiers to protect the students and integrate the school by force.

McCarthyism

Republican Senator **Joseph McCarthy**'s Communist witch hunt overshadowed all other domestic issues during Eisenhower's two terms in office. Hoping to boost his own status as a national politician, McCarthy first capitalized on Americans' fears of Communism when he announced in 1950 that the State Department had become overrun with more than 200 Communists. He claimed that these Communists, including Truman's own secretary of state, Dean Acheson, were working secretly to hinder American efforts against the Soviet Union.

Although McCarthy never offered any actual proof to back up his claims, **"McCarthyism"** swept across the nation like wildfire. Thousands of individuals, including liberals, critics of the Korean War and the Cold War, civil rights activists, homosexuals, feminists, and even critics of McCarthy himself, were blacklisted and fired from their jobs.

The Army-McCarthy Hearings

As a congressman and later as vice president, **Richard Nixon** fully supported McCarthy, as did future president **Ronald Reagan**, who at the time held the influential position of president of the Screen Actors Guild. In response to McCarthyism, author and playwright **Arthur Miller**, who had himself been branded a Communist, wrote the 1953 play *The Crucible*, a critique of the Red hunts disguised as a play about the Salem witch trials of the 1600s.

Eventually, McCarthy ruined his own name after accusing high-ranking members of the U.S. military of being Communists. During the televised **Army-McCarthy hearings** of 1954, millions of Americans watched as the senator made wild accusations without a shred of evidence. These hearings and the Senate's subsequent formal reprimand of McCarthy effectively ended the Red hunts. Disgraced and discredited, McCarthy became an alcoholic and died in 1957.

EISENHOWER AND THE COLD WAR: 1954–1960

EVENTS

1953	CIA-backed coup in Iran
1954	CIA-backed coup in Guatemala
	Dien Bien Phu falls to pro-Communist forces
	Geneva Conference splits Vietnam into two countries
	SEATO is founded
1955	Warsaw Pact is signed
1956	Suez crisis erupts
	USSR puts down Hungarian Revolution
	Eisenhower is reelected
1957	Eisenhower Doctrine is announced
	USSR launches *Sputnik I*
1958	Congress passes National Defense Education Act
1960	U-2 incident embarrasses U.S. government
1961	Eisenhower gives farewell address

KEY PEOPLE

Dwight D. Eisenhower 34th U.S. president; authorized CIA-sponsored coups abroad; committed federal funds to fighting Communists in Vietnam; resolved Suez crisis

John Foster Dulles Secretary of state who helped devise Eisenhower's New Look foreign policy, which emphasized massive retaliation with nuclear weapons; also advocated use of nuclear weapons against Ho Chi Minh in Vietnam

Allen Dulles CIA director (and brother of John Foster Dulles) who sponsored coups in Iran in 1953 and Guatemala in 1954 to install pro-American governments

Nikita Khrushchev Soviet premier who took power upon Stalin's death; seen by many observers as a moderate who might reduce Cold War tensions

Ho Chi Minh Leader of mid-1950s pro-Communist revolution in French Indochina (Vietnam) against corrupt Ngo Dinh Diem regime in Saigon

Gamal Abdel Nasser Egyptian nationalist president who seized British-controlled Suez Canal when economic aid negotiations among Egypt, Great Britain, and the United States dissolved in 1956

Mohammed Reza Shah Pahlavi Pro-American ruler who was returned to power in Iran following CIA-sponsored coup in 1953

EISENHOWER'S "NEW LOOK"

In addition to his desire to halt the advance of "creeping socialism" in U.S. domestic policy, Eisenhower also wanted to "roll back" the advances of Communism abroad. After taking office in 1953, he devised a new foreign policy tactic to contain the Soviet Union and even win back territory that had already been lost. Devised primarily by Secretary of State **John Foster Dulles**, this so-called **New Look** at foreign policy proposed the use of nuclear weapons and new technology rather than ground troops and conventional bombs, all in an effort to threaten **"massive retaliation"** against the USSR for Communist advances abroad.

In addition to intimidating the Soviet Union, this emphasis on new and cheaper weapons would also drastically reduce military spending, which had escalated rapidly during the Truman years. As a result, Eisenhower managed to stabilize defense spending, keeping it at roughly half the congressional budget during most of his eight years in office.

THE LIMITS OF MASSIVE RETALIATION
The doctrine of massive retaliation proved to be dangerously flawed, however, because it effectively left Eisenhower without any options other than nuclear war to combat Soviet aggression. This dilemma surfaced in 1956, for instance, when the Soviet Union brutally crushed a popular democratic uprising in **Hungary**. Despite Hungary's request for American recognition and military assistance, Eisenhower's hands were tied because he knew that the USSR would stop at nothing to maintain control of Eastern Europe. He could not risk turning the Cold War into a nuclear war over the interests of a small nation such as Hungary.

COVERT OPERATIONS
As an alternative, Eisenhower employed the **CIA** to tackle the specter of Communism in developing countries outside the Soviet Union's immediate sphere of influence. Newly appointed CIA director **Allen Dulles** (the secretary of state's brother) took enormous liberties in conducting a variety of **covert operations**. Thousands of CIA operatives were assigned to Africa, Asia, Latin America, and the Middle East and attempted to launch coups, assassinate heads of state, arm anti-Communist revolutionaries, spread propaganda, and support despotic pro-American regimes. Eisenhower began to favor using the CIA instead of the military because covert operations didn't attract as much attention and cost much less money.

IRAN AND GUATEMALA
A CIA-sponsored coup in **Iran** in 1953, however, did attract attention and heavy criticism from liberals both at home and in the international community. Eisenhower and the Dulles brothers authorized the coup in Iran when the Iranian government seized control of the British-owned Anglo-Iranian Oil Company. Afraid that the popular, nationalist, Soviet-friendly prime minister of Iran, **Mohammed Mossadegh**, would then cut off oil exports to the United

States, CIA operatives convinced military leaders to overthrow Mossadegh and restore **Mohammed Reza Shah Pahlavi** as head of state in 1953. Pahlavi returned control of Anglo-Iranian Oil to the British and then signed agreements to supply the United States with almost half of all the oil drilled in Iran.

The following year, a similar coup in **Guatemala** over agricultural land rights also drew international criticism and severely damaged U.S.–Latin American relations.

THE SUEZ CRISIS

In an odd twist, Eisenhower actually supported the **Communist**-leaning Egyptian president **Gamal Abdel Nasser** during the 1956 **Suez crisis**. Hoping to construct a new dam on the Nile River to provide electricity and additional land for farming, the Nationalist Nasser approached British and American officials with requests for economic assistance. When the negotiations collapsed, Nasser turned to the Soviet Union for help and then seized the British-controlled Suez Canal, which linked the Red Sea to the Mediterranean. Great Britain and France asked Eisenhower for military assistance to retake the canal, but Eisenhower refused, forcing the two powers to join with **Israel** in 1956 to retake the canal themselves. Eisenhower condemned the attack on Egypt and exerted heavy diplomatic and economic pressure on the aggressors. Unable to sustain the action in the face of U.S. disapproval and financial pressures, Great Britain and France withdrew.

THE EISENHOWER DOCTRINE

In 1957, in order to protect American oil interests in the Middle East, Eisenhower announced the **Eisenhower Doctrine**, which stated that the United States would provide military and economic assistance to Middle Eastern countries in resisting Communist insurgents. Although not terribly significant, this doctrine, as well as the restoration of Mohammed Reza Shah Pahlavi in Iran, demonstrated the growing importance of oil in American foreign policy decision making.

HO CHI MINH AND VIETNAM

A growing crisis in French **Indochina** proved to be no less challenging for Eisenhower than the Suez crisis. Ever since World War I, Vietnamese nationalists under the leadership of **Ho Chi Minh** had sought independence from France, the colonial power in the region. Although originally more nationalist and anticolonial than Communist, Ho turned to the Soviet Union in the 1950s after U.S. officials had rebuffed his earlier requests for help in securing independence. The USSR supplied money and arms to the Vietminh forces, putting Eisenhower in the difficult position of supporting a French colonial possession in order to contain the USSR.

DIEN BIEN PHU

When the key French garrison at **Dien Bien Phu** fell to Ho Chi Minh's troops in 1954, Eisenhower promised to assist the French economically. Many U.S. foreign policy thinkers feared that if one Southeast Asian country fell to Communism, all the others would fall as well, just like a row of dominoes. This so-called **domino theory** prompted Secretary of State Dulles and Vice President Nixon to advocate the use of nuclear weapons against the North Vietnamese. Remembering the fruitless war in Korea, however, Eisenhower merely responded, "I can conceive of no greater tragedy than for the United States to become engaged in all-out war in Indochina." Nevertheless, Eisenhower's financial commitment to contain Communism in Vietnam after the fall of Dien Bien Phu laid the groundwork for what eventually devolved into the Vietnam War.

THE 17TH PARALLEL

An international convention in Geneva, Switzerland, tried to avert further conflict in Vietnam by temporarily splitting the country into two countries, with the dividing line at the **17th parallel**. Ho Chi Minh erected his own government in **Hanoi** in North Vietnam, while American-supported **Ngo Dinh Diem** founded a South Vietnamese government in **Saigon**. This **Geneva Conference** agreement stipulated that the division would be only temporary, a stopgap to maintain peace until national elections could be held to reunite the country democratically.

Although the USSR consented to the agreement, Eisenhower rejected it. Instead, he pledged continued economic support to Ngo Dinh Diem and convinced Great Britain, France, Australia, and other regional nations to join the mostly symbolic **Southeast Asia Treaty Organization (SEATO)**, modeled after the highly successful NATO.

SPUTNIK AND THE SPACE RACE

In October 1957, Soviet scientists shocked the world when they announced they had successfully launched the first man-made satellite, *Sputnik I*, into orbit. They followed up on this landmark achievement several months later with the launch of *Sputnik II*. Although the satellites themselves posed no danger to the United States, Americans feared that the Soviet Union now had the ability to attack New York or Washington with nuclear-tipped intercontinental ballistic missiles, or **ICBMs**, from anywhere on the planet. In reality, the Soviet ICBM development program lagged far behind its American counterpart.

Nonetheless, the fear that the USSR would win the **"space race"** before the United States even launched its first satellite spurred Eisenhower and Congress into action. Eisenhower created the **National Aeronautics and Space Administration (NASA)** in 1958 to spearhead the American space program. Congress, meanwhile, increased defense spending and passed the **National Defense Education Act** in 1958 to fund more science and foreign language classes in public schools.

KHRUSHCHEV AND CAMP DAVID

For a brief period during Eisenhower's final years in office, it seemed that the United States and the USSR might resolve their differences peacefully and perhaps even end the Cold War. Upon Premier Joseph Stalin's death in 1953, Stalin's former enemy, **Nikita Khrushchev**, took control of the Communist Party and eventually became premier in 1956. Khrushchev denounced Stalin's brutal treatment of the Russian people and halted nuclear testing in order to divert more money to the struggling Soviet economy.

U.S.-Soviet relations also improved dramatically after Khrushchev spent two weeks touring the United States in 1959. He and Eisenhower even had a cordial meeting at the woodsy presidential retreat at **Camp David**, in Maryland. Many Americans hoped that the so-called spirit of Camp David would ease tensions between the two superpowers.

THE U-2 INCIDENT

After returning home to Moscow, Khrushchev invited Eisenhower to visit the Soviet Union and hold a multilateral summit in Paris the following year. The plans fell apart, however, after the Soviet Union shot down an American **U-2 spy plane** in 1960. Eisenhower and the U.S. government initially denied the existence of U-2 missions over the Soviet Union, but then the USSR produced the American pilot, whom they had captured alive. Embarrassed, Eisenhower refused to apologize or promise to suspend future spy missions against the USSR. The **U-2 incident** instantly repolarized the Cold

War, reversing the thaw that Khrushchev's visit had brought and forcing the abandonment of the Paris summit.

EISENHOWER'S FAREWELL

Facing a two-term limit, Eisenhower delivered his farewell address in January 1961. Ironically, he used his last speech as president to address a problem that he himself had had a hand in creating—the increasing dependence on nuclear weapons as a tool of foreign policy. By 1960, a growing number of Americans had begun to protest the United States's apparent willingness to wage nuclear warfare. Eisenhower had also begun to see nuclear weapons as more of a threat to global security than as a stabilizer. Afraid that the U.S. government and even Americans' civil liberties might succumb to the power of what he called the **"military-industrial complex,"** Eisenhower cautioned that "the potential for the disastrous rise of misplaced power exists and will persist." Although little was made of Eisenhower's words at the time, his words came back to haunt Americans during the Vietnam War.

SUMMARY & ANALYSIS

KENNEDY AND LIBERALISM: 1960–1963

EVENTS

1960	John F. Kennedy is elected president
1961	Soviet-dominated East Germany erects Berlin Wall Kennedy creates Peace Corps United States sends "military advisors" to Vietnam Bay of Pigs invasion fails
1962	Cuban missile crisis erupts
1963	Partial Nuclear Test Ban Treaty signed Washington-Moscow "hotline" established Ngo Dinh Diem is overthrown in South Vietnam Kennedy is assassinated

KEY PEOPLE

John F. Kennedy 35th U.S. president; devised tactic of "flexible response" to contain Communism; narrowly avoided Cuban missile crisis; assassinated in 1963

Richard M. Nixon Vice president under Eisenhower; lost 1960 presidential election to Kennedy

Fidel Castro Pro-Communist revolutionary who seized power in Cuba in 1959; formed alliance with USSR that led to Cuban missile crisis of 1962

Ngo Dinh Diem Ruler of South Vietnam after Geneva Conference split country at 17th parallel; overthrown and executed in 1963

Nikita Khrushchev Soviet premier during Cuban missile crisis; was removed by Communist Party leaders for having backed down during the crisis

Lee Harvey Oswald Man who assassinated Kennedy in November 1963 in Dallas, Texas

THE ELECTION OF 1960

With Eisenhower out of the running, Republicans nominated Vice President **Richard M. Nixon** at their national nominating convention in 1960. Conservatives loved the former Red hunter for his tough-talking stance against Communism and the Soviet Union. As vice president, Nixon had traveled abroad extensively to handle "brush-fire" crises and had even engaged Khrushchev in a televised debate in Moscow. Democrats, meanwhile, nominated the relatively unknown **John F. Kennedy**, a young but accomplished senator from Massachusetts who had served with distinction in World War II and had won a Pulitzer Prize for his 1956 book *Profiles in Courage*.

At only forty-three years old, Kennedy exuded a youthful confidence that contrasted sharply with Nixon's serious demeanor—a contrast that was plainly evident in the first-ever live **televised presidential debates** in 1960. Tens of millions of Americans tuned in to watch the two candidates discuss the issues. Although radio listeners might have concluded that Nixon "won" the debates, Kennedy took full advantage of the visual television medium by projecting strength, coolness, and even cheerfulness, whereas Nixon appeared nervous, pale, and shaken on-screen. Largely thanks to these TV debates, Kennedy defeated Nixon by a slim margin to become the youngest and first Catholic president.

THE NEW FRONTIER

During his campaign, Kennedy had promised voters to revive government **liberalism**, which had withered under Eisenhower, with a new set of reforms collectively called the **New Frontier**. The young president wanted to expand Social Security to benefit more Americans, help the elderly pay their medical costs, fund educational endeavors, raise the national minimum wage, and reduce income inequality.

In his famous inaugural address, Kennedy appealed to American youth by instructing them to "ask not what your country can do for you; ask what you can do for your country." He later launched the **Peace Corps** to support this effort, encouraging young Americans to assist people in developing countries. Kennedy also responded to national fears and pressures regarding the space race with the Soviet Union by challenging Americans to put a **man on the moon** by the end of the decade. His enthusiasm spread across the country.

CHALLENGES TO LIBERALISM

Despite these enthusiastic promises and a great amount of public support, Kennedy achieved only a few of his goals because conservative southern Democrats united with Republicans in Congress to block almost all New Frontier legislation. Congress did raise the minimum wage to $1.25 per hour and funneled a little more money into Social Security, but it refused to pass any major reforms.

THE BERLIN WALL

Kennedy's first foreign policy crisis surfaced just months after he took office, when Soviet premier **Nikita Khrushchev** threatened to sign a treaty with East Germany that would cut off the city of **Berlin** from the United States and Western Europe. Although the Soviet Union never signed any such treaty, it did construct a massive wall of concrete and barbed wire around West Berlin in 1961 to prevent East Germans from escaping to freedom in the Western-controlled part of the city. Over the years, guard towers were installed, and the "no-man's-land" between the inner and outer walls was mined and booby-trapped, making it incredibly difficult for East Germans to escape to West Berlin without being killed or captured. Over the ensuing decades, the **Berlin Wall** came to be the most famous symbol of the Cold War.

DECOLONIZATION

During Kennedy's term, the issue of **decolonization** posed a particularly difficult problem for a U.S. government committed to halting the spread of Communism. As more and more new, independent countries were formed from old European colonies in Africa, Asia, and the Middle East, Kennedy faced an increasingly difficult task of ensuring that Communists did not seize power. Complicating the situation was the fact that Eisenhower's stated policy of "massive retaliation," which threatened to use nuclear weapons to halt the Communist tide, effectively tied the president's hands. On one hand, Kennedy would lose credibility if he allowed Communism to take root in any of these newly decolonized countries. At the same time, however, he wanted to do anything he could to avoid using nuclear weapons.

The growing Communist power in the Southeast Asian country of **Laos** made this catch-22 very real. After carefully considering his options, Kennedy finally decided not to use military force and instead convened a multination peace conference in Geneva in 1962 to end the civil war that had erupted in Laos.

"FLEXIBLE RESPONSE"

Kennedy, hoping never to have to decide between nuclear war and political embarrassment again, devised a new strategy of **"flexible response"** to deal with the USSR. Crafted with the aid of foreign policy veteran Defense Secretary **Robert S. McNamara**, the flexible response doctrine was meant to allow the president to combat Soviet advances around the world through a variety of means. In other words, Kennedy could send money or troops to fight Communist insurgents, authorize the CIA to topple an unfriendly government, or, as a last resort, use nuclear weapons.

COMMITMENT IN VIETNAM

Kennedy first applied his new doctrine to the problem in **Vietnam**, which was becoming an even greater problem than Laos had been. The United States had been funding **Ngo Dinh Diem**'s corrupt South Vietnamese regime since Eisenhower first pledged support after the fall of Dien Bien Phu in 1954. Most South Vietnamese, however, hated Diem, resented the United States for keeping him in power, and threatened to overthrow him on numerous occasions.

To prevent Communist-backed insurgents from taking control of South Vietnam, Kennedy increased American commitment by sending approximately 15,000 U.S. servicemen to Saigon, ostensibly as mere **"military advisors."** When anti-Diem sentiment continued to intensify, however, the United States supported exactly what it had tried to prevent—it allowed a 1963 **coup** to overthrow Diem.

Kennedy's decision to send "military advisors" to South Vietnam drastically increased U.S. involvement in the Vietnamese civil war. Eisenhower, after all, had merely funded the anti-Communist faction, just as Truman had funded such factions in Greece and Turkey in the late 1940s. Because the United States sent troops, regardless of what they were called, responsibility for the war began to shift away from South Vietnam and onto the United States. The arrival of the first group of soldiers in Vietnam opened the floodgates, and additional troops soon followed. Eventually, Kennedy and future presidents would find it politically impossible to recall U.S. forces without having first defeated the pro-Communist North Vietnamese. Kennedy's decision to send "military advisors" ultimately proved to be a costly mistake that entangled the United States in what would prove to be the longest and least successful war in American history to date. (*For more information, see the History SparkNote* The Vietnam War.)

THE ALLIANCE FOR PROGRESS
In **Latin America**, Kennedy used a different strategy to fight Communist forces. Hoping to reduce income inequality and quell pro-Communist stirrings in Central America, South America, and the Caribbean, Kennedy decided in 1961 to give hundreds of millions of dollars in grants to the region's nations. This so-called **Alliance for Progress** had very little real effect. Although Democrats lauded the alliance as the Marshall Plan for the Western Hemisphere, the money did almost nothing to reduce the Latin American poverty rate.

THE BAY OF PIGS INVASION
Hoping to topple **Cuba**'s Communist-leaning leader, **Fidel Castro**, Kennedy authorized the CIA to train and arm pro-American Cuban exiles and support them in an attempted invasion of Cuba in 1961. U.S. foreign policy advisors hoped that the American-armed exiles, with U.S. Air Force support, could overpower Castro's sentries and spark a popular uprising.

Shortly before the invasion, however, Kennedy privately decided not to commit to U.S. air support. The CIA-trained exiles, believing that American planes would cover them, stormed a beach on Cuba's **Bay of Pigs** in April 1961, only to be ruthlessly gunned down by Castro's forces. The invasion was a complete failure and an embarrassment for the Kennedy administration and the United States. Kennedy accepted full responsibility for the massacre but continued to authorize covert CIA missions to assassinate Castro, all of which proved unsuccessful.

THE CUBAN MISSILE CRISIS

The following year, the true cost of the Bay of Pigs fiasco became apparent, and it turned out to be even worse than it had initially appeared. Castro, understandably outraged at the U.S. attempt to oust him, turned to the Soviet Union for support. Khrushchev, eager to have an ally so close to U.S. shores, readily welcomed Castro's friendship. In 1962, it was revealed that the USSR had installed several **nuclear missiles** in Cuba, less than 100 miles off the Florida coast.

Upon learning of the missiles' existence, a stunned Kennedy ordered the U.S. Navy to **blockade** Cuba and demanded that Khrushchev remove the missiles. Moreover, he threatened to retaliate against Moscow if Cuba launched any missiles at the United States. With neither side willing to concede, the world stood on the brink of all-out nuclear war for nearly two weeks. Finally, Khrushchev offered to remove the missiles if the United States ended the blockade. Kennedy quickly agreed and likewise offered to remove from Turkey American nuclear warheads aimed at the USSR. The **Cuban missile crisis** was the closest the United States and the Soviet Union came to nuclear war during the Cold War era.

COOLING OFF

Because neither Washington, D.C., nor Moscow actually wanted a nuclear holocaust, they agreed to install a **"hotline"** between the two capitals so that the Soviet premier and the U.S. president could speak to each other personally during future crises. The Communist Party leadership in the USSR also removed Khrushchev from power for having made the first concession to end the crisis. Meanwhile, Kennedy pressured the Soviets to sign the **Partial Nuclear Test Ban Treaty** in 1963 to outlaw atmospheric and underwater detonation tests. Although the treaty was mostly a symbolic gesture, as it did not prohibit underground tests, it nevertheless marked a key step toward reducing tensions between the United States and the USSR.

KENNEDY'S ASSASSINATION

Kennedy's presidency came to a tragic and unexpected end on November 22, 1963, while the president was riding in a motorcade in Dallas, Texas. Armed with a rifle and hiding in a nearby book depository, assassin **Lee Harvey Oswald** shot Kennedy as his convertible passed. Vice President **Lyndon Johnson** was sworn in as Kennedy's successor later that day. Although Oswald was arrested within an hour and a half of the assassination, he himself was shot and killed two days later in a Dallas police station (and on live television) by another gunman, named **Jack Ruby**.

Conspiracy theories about the assassination arose almost immediately after Oswald's death. A week after he took office, President Johnson formed the **Warren Commission**, headed by Chief Justice of the Supreme Court **Earl Warren**, to launch an official investigation into Kennedy's death. Although the commission's report ultimately concluded that Oswald acted alone, it did little to silence the claims of conspiracy theorists. Another congressional investigation in 1979 questioned the Warren Commission's findings, and speculation continues to this day.

SUMMARY & ANALYSIS

STUDY QUESTIONS & ESSAY TOPICS

Always use specific historical examples to support your arguments.

STUDY QUESTIONS

Although both Truman and Stalin helped increase tensions in Europe and East Asia in the years immediately following World War II, the Cold War itself was likely inevitable. The alliance that had formed between the United States and the USSR during World War II was not strong enough to overcome the past decades of suspicion and unease between the two nations. Moreover, as both leaders sought to achieve their postwar security objectives, which were often mutually exclusive, neither was willing to compromise.

The United States and the USSR had always generally disliked and distrusted each other, despite the fact that they were allies against Germany and Japan during the war. Americans had hated and feared Communism ever since it had appeared in the Bolshevik Revolution of 1917 and had refused to recognize the new Soviet government, especially after Bolshevik leaders promoted the destruction of capitalism. During World War II, Roosevelt and British prime minister Winston Churchill delayed their decision to open a second front, which would have distracted the Nazis and taken pressure off the Red Army entrenched at Stalingrad. Stalin resented this delay, just as he resented the fact that the United States and Great Britain refused to share their nuclear weapons research with the Soviet Union. After the war, Truman's decision to give Great Britain relief loans while denying similar requests from the USSR only added to the resentment.

Another major factor contributing to the Cold War was the fact that the United States and USSR were the only two powers to escape World War II relatively unharmed. Whereas other major world powers such as Great Britain, France, Italy, and Germany lay in ruins, the Soviet Union and the United States still had manufactur-

QUESTIONS & ESSAYS

ing and military capabilities. The world had been a multipolar one before the war but was bipolar afterward, and this new order implicitly pitted the already distrustful and ideologically opposed United States and Soviet Union against each other.

Perhaps most important, both powers had conflicting security goals that neither wanted to concede. The USSR, which had already been invaded twice in the first half of the twentieth century, wanted to set up friendly governments throughout Eastern Europe to create a buffer between Moscow and Germany. In addition to exacting enormous war reparations, Stalin wanted to dismantle German factories to keep Germany weak and dependent. Truman, conversely, believed that rebuilding, reindustrializing, and democratizing Europe was the key to preventing another world war. With neither side willing to compromise on these conflicting ideologies and postwar plans, tension between the United States and the USSR was inevitable.

2. *Why has the Korean War often been called America's "forgotten war"? What purpose did the war serve, and what impact did it have?*

The Korean War has often been called America's "forgotten war" because the United States made no significant territorial or political gains during the war. Despite the fact that tens of thousands of Americans died, the war both began and ended with the Korean Peninsula divided at the 38th parallel. Nevertheless, the Korean War helped define the Cold War, established a precedent for keeping peripheral wars limited, and boosted defense spending that contributed to the postwar economic boom in the United States.

Despite the loss of life, the Korean War faded from national memory, perhaps because the three-year conflict ended without any territorial or political gains. Although General Douglas MacArthur captured nearly the entire Korean Peninsula after his brilliant Inchon landing, his tactical miscalculation at the Yalu River brought China into the war and forced United Nations troops back down to the 38th parallel, where they had started. Both sides became entrenched there, each preventing the other from making any headway. As a result, neither side could claim victory when cease-fire negotiations began in 1953. The 38th parallel remained one of the "hottest" Cold War borders in the world, almost as if the war had never really ended.

The Korean War was an important conflict, however, because it set the tone for the entire Cold War. In expanding the draft and sending more than 3 million U.S. troops to Korea, Truman demonstrated to the USSR his commitment to containing Communism at almost any cost. This demonstration of massive U.S. military force in East Asia forced the Soviets to rethink postwar policy in Eastern Europe and the rest of Asia.

Truman also set a precedent during the war of avoiding the use of nuclear weapons, despite the fact that MacArthur advocated using them against North Koreans and the Chinese. Although the American public vilified Truman for this decision and for firing his insubordinate general, the decision proved to be prudent. The president knew that using nuclear weapons would only drag the Soviet Union and China fully into the conflict, which would destabilize Europe and initiate a third world war—one that might even lead to all-out nuclear war. By refusing to use nuclear weapons, Truman kept the war confined to the Korean Peninsula. The decision would later have an enormous impact on future presidents making similar decisions in Vietnam. Truman's actions in Korea therefore demonstrated not only American resolve to contain Communism but also a desire to keep the Cold War from devolving into an open war.

The Korean War also boosted American military spending, as a result of a memorandum issued by the National Security Council, known as NSC-68. The memo recommended that Congress quadruple military and defense spending in order to contain the Soviet Union. As a result, the percentage of Congress's annual budget spent on defense soared throughout the following years, hovering at roughly 50 percent under the Eisenhower administration. Government investment in war factories kept employment high and money flowing into the economy between 1950 and 1970, contributing significantly to the prosperous economic boom.

3. *Was the United States, the USSR, or Cuba more to blame for the Cuban missile crisis? What impact did the crisis have on U.S.-Soviet relations?*

Because the United States attempted repeatedly to assassinate or overthrow Fidel Castro in the early 1960s, the blame for the resulting Cuban missile crisis falls squarely on American shoulders. Had it not been for Khrushchev's ultimate willingness to back down and end the crisis, the United States and the USSR might actually have ended up in the nuclear war that the world feared.

The United States tried repeatedly to topple Castro after he seized power in a popularly supported revolution in Cuba in 1959. Americans disliked the Castro regime because it threatened U.S. economic interests in the country. When the United States withdrew its financial support from Castro's government, Castro turned to the Soviet Union for assistance. In order to prevent Cuba's Communist influence from spreading throughout Latin America, Kennedy launched the Alliance for Progress, a program that awarded Latin American countries millions of dollars in U.S. aid to tackle poverty. Kennedy took more direct action when he authorized the arming and training of 1,200 anti-Castro Cuban exiles to invade the island, in the hopes that the invasion would cause a massive public uprising that would ultimately depose Castro. The plan for this Bay of Pigs invasion failed, however, when Kennedy decided not to involve American military forces and withheld the air support he had previously promised the exiles. As a result, the Cuban army killed or captured all of the exiles, and the invasion attempt was an embarrassment for the U.S. government.

Although Kennedy accepted full responsibility for the Bay of Pigs failure, he continued to authorize unsuccessful CIA-led assassination attempts against Castro. Not surprisingly, Castro turned to the Soviet Union for support, and in 1962, U.S. intelligence officials discovered that the Soviet Union had placed nuclear missiles in Cuba. Kennedy sent a naval blockade to circle the island, despite Cuban and Soviet protests, and refused to back down, even at the risk of nuclear war. The crisis ended only when Khrushchev himself agreed to remove the missiles in exchange for an end to the blockade. This sacrifice cost him his position as head of the Soviet Communist Party but saved the world from the prospect of nuclear war between the superpowers.

The crisis had a significant impact on U.S.-Soviet relations, as both sides worked to improve their relationship in order to prevent another potentially catastrophic situation from arising. A Moscow-Washington "hotline," for example, was installed so that the Soviet premier and American president could speak to each other personally should another crisis occur. Kennedy also changed his rhetoric by asking Americans to think more kindly of the Russians rather than see them as enemies. He also pushed the USSR into signing the Partial Nuclear Test Ban Treaty, a symbolic but nonetheless significant step that helped pave the way for détente in the 1970s.

SUGGESTED ESSAY TOPICS

1. *How did George Kennan's containment doctrine change during the Truman, Eisenhower and Kennedy administrations? Which president was the most successful in containing Communism?*

2. *What were the causes of the American economic boom in the 1950s? How did prosperity affect the nation socially, politically, and economically?*

3. *Why were Americans so terrified of Communist infiltration after World War II? What impact did the Red hunts of the late 1940s and early 1950s have on American politics and society?*

4. *What impact did the Korean War have on American foreign policy?*

5. *Why was the launch of Sputnik I in 1957 so significant? What did its launch mean for Americans?*

REVIEW & RESOURCES

QUIZ

1. Joseph McCarthy's political influence waned after

   A. The Rosenbergs were wrongfully executed
   B. The House Un-American Activities Committee found no evidence of Communists infiltrating the U.S. State Department
   C. The Army-McCarthy hearings
   D. He accused Eisenhower's wife of being a Communist

2. In both the 1950s and 1960s, national income approximately

   A. Doubled
   B. Tripled
   C. Quadrupled
   D. Quintupled

3. What did the Montgomery G.I. Bill do?

   A. Reinstated the draft after the Korean War erupted
   B. Gave money to World War II veterans to go to school
   C. Provided disabled veterans with government pensions
   D. All of the above

4. America's postwar economic prosperity was the result of all of the following *except*

   A. The Montgomery G.I. Bill
   B. Continued American military spending
   C. The development of agribusiness
   D. The creation of the World Bank

5. Truman fired General MacArthur for

    A. Failing to retake South Korea
    B. Failing to take all of Korea
    C. Suggesting the use of nuclear weapons against North Korea and China
    D. Publicly criticizing Truman

6. What was the Marshall Plan intended to do?

    A. Rebuild war-ravaged Europe
    B. Rescue starving Berliners behind a Soviet blockade
    C. Unify the U.S. armed forces
    D. Give more powers to the president to root out Communist spies in the United States

7. Why did Truman ignore his advisors and officially recognize Israel as a new and independent nation in 1948?

    A. He wanted Jewish-American votes
    B. The American public sympathized with Jews after the Holocaust
    C. He wanted to keep the USSR out of Israel
    D. All of the above

8. The imaginary line of secrecy and mistrust that separated the USSR and Eastern Europe from the West was known as

    A. The iron curtain
    B. The Berlin Wall
    C. NATO
    D. The Warsaw Pact

9. The United States and the USSR distrusted each other after World War II for all of the following reasons *except*

   A. The United States had hesitated to open a second front during the war to help save the Soviet Union from a German invasion
   B. The United States had granted postwar loans to Great Britain but not to the USSR
   C. The United States and Great Britain had not shared nuclear research with the Soviet Union during the war
   D. The United States and Great Britain had wanted to assassinate Stalin during the war

10. For which disease did Jonas Salk discover a vaccine in 1954?

    A. Tetanus
    B. Polio
    C. Whooping cough
    D. Tuberculosis

11. Arthur Miller's play *The Crucible*, set in seventeenth-century New England, was actually a critique of

    A. The Korean War
    B. Conservatism
    C. McCarthyism
    D. Communism and totalitarianism

12. How did the Taft-Hartley Act hurt organized labor?

    A. By outlawing all-union shops
    B. By holding unions responsible for damages incurred during disputes between unions
    C. By making union leaders take loyalty oaths
    D. All of the above

13. In which U.S. presidential election did television first play a major role?

    A. 1948
    B. 1952
    C. 1956
    D. 1960

REVIEW & RESOURCES

14. Kennedy's doctrine of "flexible response"

   A. Forbade the use of nuclear weapons during the Cold War
   B. Allowed foreign policy officials to use a range of strategies to fight Communists abroad, depending on the crisis
   C. Justified the recognition of Israel as an independent country
   D. Promised to defend Western Europe from nations in the Eastern bloc

15. At which parallel did delegates at the Geneva Conference divide North and South Vietnam?

   A. The 38th parallel
   B. The 17th parallel
   C. The 45th parallel
   D. The 10th parallel

16. The Soviet Union's brutal response to the 1956 Hungarian Revolution demonstrated the ineffectiveness of the U.S. strategy of

   A. Flexible response
   B. Massive retaliation
   C. Containment
   D. The Truman Doctrine

17. The CIA orchestrated a coup against the government of Iran and restored the pro-American ruler in 1953 because of

   A. Threats by the Iranian government against the United States
   B. U.S. fear of Soviet interference in the oil-rich Middle East
   C. The Iran hostage crisis
   D. The Iran-Contra affair

18. Why did Great Britain, France, and Israel launch a surprise attack on Egypt in 1956?

   A. Egyptian president Nasser seized control of the Suez Canal
   B. Egypt had fallen under control of the Soviet Union
   C. Egypt claimed to have nuclear weapons
   D. Egypt was preparing to invade Israel

19. Eisenhower cut many federally funded government programs in order to curb what he called

   A. "Creeping socialism"
   B. "Conservatism"
   C. The "military-industrial complex"
   D. "McCarthyism"

20. The fall of the French garrison at Dien Bien Phu in 1954 prompted

   A. Kennedy to send U.S. "military advisors" to South Vietnam
   B. Eisenhower to funnel U.S. funds into fighting Communist-leaning North Vietnamese
   C. Lyndon Johnson to send 500,000 U.S. troops to Vietnam
   D. South Vietnam ruler Ngo Dinh Diem to abdicate

21. The United States tried unsuccessfully to unite pro-U.S. Southeast Asia together under

   A. The Warsaw Pact
   B. The Alliance for Progress
   C. NATO
   D. SEATO

22. Which Kennedy initiative hoped to thwart Communist insurgents in Latin America by reducing income inequality in the region?

A. The Alliance for Progress
B. The Marshall Plan
C. The Good Neighbor policy
D. The Warsaw Pact

23. All of the following were consequences of the Cuban missile crisis *except*

A. The USSR removed its nuclear warheads from Cuba
B. The United States removed its nuclear warheads from Turkey
C. Kennedy authorized the Bay of Pigs invasion
D. Khrushchev was removed from power in the USSR

24. The United States and the USSR came closest to nuclear war during the

A. Korean War
B. Suez crisis
C. Cuban missile crisis
D. Berlin crisis

25. What did Kennedy's New Frontier program seek to do?

A. Increase social welfare spending
B. Decrease military spending
C. Halt "creeping socialism"
D. Fund anti-Communist insurgents abroad

26. The belief that the United States had to prevent the USSR from expanding and Communism from spreading was known as

A. Creeping socialism
B. Massive retaliation
C. Containment
D. The Marshall Plan

27. In which country or countries was the Truman Doctrine first put to the test in 1947?

    A. Turkey and Greece
    B. Egypt
    C. China
    D. Berlin

28. Why did the USSR vehemently oppose the Marshall Plan?

    A. It wanted to strengthen Japan first
    B. It wanted to strengthen China first
    C. It feared invasion from a newly industrialized Germany
    D. It wanted the money for its own domestic concerns

29. NSC-68 proposed that the U.S. government should

    A. Abandon the containment doctrine
    B. Quadruple military spending
    C. Use nuclear weapons
    D. Attack the USSR

30. Why did Truman veto the McCarran Internal Security Bill?

    A. He feared it stripped Americans of many civil liberties
    B. He didn't think the bill gave enough power to the president
    C. He thought it would increase military spending too much
    D. He thought security should be left to the individual state governments

31. What did Republicans in the House of Representatives create in order to hunt for Communist spies?

    A. NATO
    B. HUAC
    C. The NSA
    D. The CIA

REVIEW & RESOURCES

32. Future president Richard Nixon became nationally prominent in the late 1940s when he

 A. Criticized Truman for not using nuclear weapons against China
 B. Resolved the Berlin crisis
 C. Prosecuted Alger Hiss
 D. Became the controversial first director of the CIA

33. The Red hunt and McCarthyism in the early 1950s were prompted by all of the following *except*

 A. The fall of China to Communists
 B. The USSR's development of the H-bomb
 C. The Berlin crisis
 D. The U-2 incident

34. Why was NATO created?

 A. To prevent another world war
 B. To root out Communist spies in the federal government
 C. To contain the USSR
 D. To unite the Western powers against possible invasion by the USSR

35. The Warsaw Pact was signed

 A. To unite the Western powers against possible invasion by the Soviet Union
 B. To create an Eastern bloc alliance to counter NATO
 C. Between the USSR and Cuba after the American-backed Bay of Pigs invasion
 D. To unite pro-American nations in Southeast Asia against Communism

36. What did the National Security Act of 1947 do?

 A. Created the Central Intelligence Agency
 B. United the U.S. armed forces under the Secretary of Defense
 C. Established the National Security Council to advise the president
 D. All of the above

37. Who said, "It must be the policy of the United States to support free peoples who are resisting attempted subjugation by armed minorities or by outside pressures"?

    A.   Dwight D. Eisenhower
    B.   Harry S Truman
    C.   John F. Kennedy
    D.   Richard M. Nixon

38. The Soviet satellite *Sputnik I* scared Americans because they feared that the USSR

    A.   Would put men on the moon first
    B.   Could launch nuclear ICBMs
    C.   Would put the first man into space
    D.   Would build the first armored space station

39. What incident ruined the 1960 Paris summit between Eisenhower and Khrushchev?

    A.   The Suez crisis
    B.   The Berlin crisis
    C.   The U-2 incident
    D.   The fall of Dien Bien Phu

40. The collapse of Ngo Dinh Diem's regime in South Vietnam prompted Kennedy to

    A.   Bomb North Vietnam
    B.   Authorize the Bay of Pigs invasion
    C.   Form the Alliance for Progress
    D.   Send American troops to South Vietnam

41. The leader of nationalist, Communist forces in Vietnam in the 1950s was

    A.   Mao Zedong
    B.   Chiang Kai-shek
    C.   Ho Chi Minh
    D.   Ngo Dinh Diem

REVIEW & RESOURCES

42. The Eisenhower Doctrine was aimed at bolstering key nations from Communist insurgents in

    A.   The Middle East
    B.   Latin America
    C.   Southeast Asia
    D.   Western Europe

43. What did the Eisenhower Doctrine demonstrate?

    A.   Eisenhower's commitment to spreading democracy around the world
    B.   The growing importance of oil in American foreign policy
    C.   Eisenhower's willingness to use nuclear weapons
    D.   All of the above

44. Why did Great Britain and France halt their attack on Egypt in 1956?

    A.   The USSR threatened to destroy London and Paris with nuclear ICBMs
    B.   Egypt threatened to destroy the Suez Canal
    C.   The United States condemned the act and placed political and economic pressure on both countries
    D.   Islamic militants threatened to launch a holy war

45. Julius and Ethel Rosenberg

    A.   Were the only Americans ever convicted of being Communists
    B.   Were the first Americans civilians executed for espionage
    C.   Leaked information on nuclear weapons technology to China
    D.   Were prosecuted by Joseph McCarthy

46. Truman's liberal domestic policies were collectively
    known as the

    A. Fair Deal
    B. Square Deal
    C. New Deal
    D. Bum Deal

47. Along with the United States and Great Britain, all of the
    following nations were given permanent seats on the
    powerful United Nations Security Council *except*

    A. France
    B. China
    C. The USSR
    D. Japan

48. Who constituted the bulk of the Bay of Pigs invasion force?

    A. Cuban exiles and expatriates
    B. CIA operatives and Green Berets
    C. UN peacekeepers
    D. NATO soldiers

49. Cuban leader Fidel Castro allowed the USSR to place nuclear
    missiles in Cuba after

    A. Kennedy formed the Alliance for Progress
    B. NATO was formed
    C. The Bay of Pigs invasion
    D. The U-2 incident

50. The Cold War was fought between the United States and

    A.   China

    B.   Canada

    C.   The USSR

    D.   Germany

Suggestions for Further Reading

DICKSON, PAUL. *Sputnik: The Shock of the Century.* New York: Walker, 2001.

FREEDMAN, LAWRENCE. *Kennedy's Wars: Berlin, Cuba, Laos, and Vietnam.* New York: Oxford University Press, 2000.

FRIED, ALBERT. *McCarthyism: The Great American Red Scare.* New York: Oxford University Press, 1996.

GADDIS, JOHN LEWIS. *The United States and the Origins of the Cold War.* New York: Columbia University Press, 2000.

———. *We Now Know: Rethinking Cold War History.* New York: Oxford University Press, 1997.

JENSEN, KENNETH M. *The Origins of the Cold War: The Novikov, Kennan, and Roberts "Long Telegrams" of 1946.* Washington, D.C.: United States Institute of Peace, 1993.

MCCULLOUGH, DAVID. *Truman.* New York: Simon & Schuster, 1992.

PIERPAOLI, PAUL G., JR. *Truman and Korea: The Political Culture of the Early Cold War.* Columbia: University of Missouri Press, 1999.